REDWOODS IRON HORSES AND THE PACIFIC

The Story of the California Western "SKUNK" Railroad

CALIFORNIA WESTERN — THE REDWOOD ROUTE

Also by Spencer Crump:

Ride the Big Red Cars
How Trolleys Helped Build Southern California

California's Spanish Missions Yesterday and Today

252 Historic Places You Can See in California

Black Riot in Los Angeles
The Story of the Watts Tragedy

Henry Huntington and the Pacific Electric
A Pictorial Album

PHOTOGRAPH BY RICHARD DATIN

Skunk in the Redwoods

REDWOODS, IRON HORSES, AND THE PACIFIC

The Story of the California Western "Skunk" Railroad

by SPENCER CRUMP

TRANS-ANGLO BOOKS

Redwoods, Iron Horses, and The Pacific:

The Story of the California Western "SKUNK" Railroad

THIRD EDITION (REVISED)

Copyright © MCMLXIII, MCMLXV, and MCMLXXI
by Spencer Crump
Library of Congress Catalog No. 76-114735

ISBN: 0-87046-021-8

Printed and Bound in the United States of America

Published by Trans-Anglo Books,
Post Office Box 1771, Costa Mesa, California 92626

FRONTISPIECE: The "Super Skunk" steam train and Skunk M-300 pose after loading passengers for the scenic Redwood Route trip. (Photograph by Ed Frietas)

The hostess on The Super Skunk steam train is garbed in an attractive "Skunk" costume. This hostess poses by the California Western station in Fort Bragg.

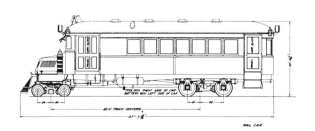

Dedicated to My Wife

MARY DALGARNO CRUMP

Who Also Likes Redwoods and Railroads

The author, Spencer Crump, talks with his children, Victoria Elizabeth Margaret and John Spencer, after riding over The Skunk Route.

The California Western's acquisition of two powerful Baldwin locomotives, Nos. 22 (left) and 21, inspired this photograph to compare them with an engine used in the late nineteenth century. The small locomotive was used by the Glen Blair Lumber Company, whose tracks connected to the CWR.

Introduction

The conductor calls a happy "all aboard." The train rolls from the depot, carrying its passengers into the redwood forest and stopping at picturesque little stations shaded by the big trees. The train winds around mountains and goes through tunnels.

This isn't a scene from the glory days of railroading a half century ago, but present day activity on the California Western Railroad. The line stretches from Fort Bragg to Willits through scenery that is among the most beautiful in the world.

The CWR is a living passenger railway. Although technically classified as a short line, it is reaching out for the fame reserved for big railroads.

Part of this latter day glory accorded the California Western can be credited to its picturesque "Skunk" rail buses. Much of its fame, however, stems from the line's scenic beauty that appropriately provides its slogan, "The Redwood Route."

This book endeavors to recount the history of the California Western Railroad.

The CWR's importance is twofold.

First, the California Western helps preserve a heritage that played a major role in building America. It was the railroads whose steel highways brought settlers from the eastern seaboard where the nation's population first was concentrated.

This heritage of carefree rail travel apparently is vanishing despite its comfort and safety. (The National Safety Council reports that the ratio of passenger deaths per 100 million miles of travel is .2 on trains, .62 on scheduled airplanes, and a staggering 2.7 in automobiles. What is more, there are fewer scenic beauties viewed from speeding planes than trains that travel reasonably fast.) Unfortunately passenger service is unprofitable to most railroads, faced with the law of economics that it takes money to remain in business.

The California Western preserves a taste of this earlier and more leisurely way of life for those who have cherished rail travel and for the generations generally deprived of this pleasure.

Railroads through the incomparable redwoods are particularly nostalgic. The author vividly recalls his first train ride, a happy experience that came when he was three years old. His mother, Jessie Person Crump, took him on a Sunday outing aboard the Southern Pacific from his native San Jose. The train rolled through the magnificent redwoods to seaside Santa Cruz (where the author had a fling at every ride, including an unforgettable miniature train).

This steam train route to Santa Cruz is no more, but memories of it are flamed by the California Western — which still rolls and recalls bygone train rides to others.

Secondly, the CWR is of interest because it has utilized the Skunk rail buses, capturing the imagination of riders because they are akin to both trolleys and conventional trains.

More important, the rail buses helped the California Western reduce operating costs that were encountered with conventional trains of locomotives and passenger coaches.

Other railroads in the United States might learn an economic lesson from the Skunks, each of which is a train in itself.

Use of such passenger equipment containing individual power plants would go far in reducing capital outlays for rolling stock as well as slashing operating costs. Such action could save the remaining American rail passenger service from disappearing under the impact of excessive costs.

The general rescue of railroad passenger service nationally would go far in solving the never-ending automotive freeway and turnpike construction programs that are so costly.

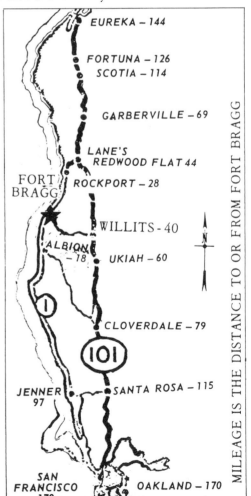

6

The tensions and dangers of highway and freeway driving are forcing more people back to railroad travel. More passengers can be lured by frequent service that could be afforded by rail buses and other improvements.

The author during the research and writing of this book relied completely on trolleys, buses, and trains for travel, much to his comfort and relaxation — not to speak of opportunities for reading or enjoying conversations with other passengers.

While this book seeks to recall the colorful days when the California Western was born, grew, and launched its rail bus service, it does not intend to serve as a history of its parent firm, The Union Lumber Company. Neither does it attempt to study the economic or social aspects of logging. Competent studies have made and are continuing to make such endeavors.

The author expresses his thanks to many individuals and organizations for assistance in the research and other preparation of this volume.

C. Russell Johnson, grandson of the founder of The Union Lumber Company and now its president as well as vice president of the California Western, made company records and historical pictures available.

While many executives in similar positions would have sought praise for their companies and products, Mr. Johnson made only one request. He asked that adequate recognition be given in this book to the rank and file CWR employees who helped give the railroad its personality.

An effort to do exactly this has been made. If intimates of the California Western note the omission of familiar names, it is only because records too frequently concern themselves with statistics relative to equipment and finances rather than the personalities so important for making a railroad as friendly as the CWR.

Among the veteran employees who not only operated Western but helped make it a friendly railroad are Fred Goranson and Edward Hendrickson, engineers; Thorne W. Holmes, superintendent of maintenance of ways and structures; Matt Lehtimaki, bridge foreman; Thomas Golden, Art Hanson, Walter Saunders, Candido Nunes, and John A. Cummings, conductors; Pete Cimolino, section foreman, and Claude King, dispatcher.

A special word of thanks goes to three veteran California Western employees: Wharton Taylor, Fred Hanson, and John Pimentel. Although maturing in years, they are young in spirit and alert in their recollections of railroading's glory days.

Mr. Taylor lived in the redwoods near Fort Bragg as a boy and hiked along the CWR roadbed before the rails were laid. He later became the railroad's general traffic agent.

Mr. Hanson went to work for the CWR in 1906. He served as conductor on the first passenger train to roll from Fort Bragg to Willits. He became the CWR's superintendent of transportation before retiring in 1950.

John Pimentel came to America from his native Azores as a youth, fell in love with the redwoods, and stayed to work for the California Western. He helped lay track before becoming a trainman and serving as brakeman on the first train to Willits.

Many present-day employees of the CWR were most helpful in gathering material, and it is unfortunate that space does not permit naming them all.

Clair W. MacLeod, president of the California Western, and F. H. Sturges, vice president and general manager, offered fine co-operation. R. A. Regalia, CWR assistant general manager and auditor, was extremely helpful in assembling data.

Other CWR personnel who aided in this study include Vernon Hanson, trainmaster; Henry A. Foltz, general traffic agent; Lawrence M. Weller, agent; William Schatz, dispatcher, and Esther Beccaria, secretary-clerk in the auditor's office.

Gratitude also goes to Mrs. Howard (Marjorie) McLure, whose father, H. H. Sanborn, was a former CWR president; Amel T. Nelson, associated with the railroad from 1919 to 1958 first as clerk and finally as vice president and general manager, and R. P. Meehan of Watson and Meehan, who provided field reports and data relative to mechanical aspects of the CWR rail buses and also made pictures available.

W. R. Shanks and Robert Smith, publisher and editor respectively of the Fort Bragg Advocate-News, graciously made early day files of the newspaper available at the author's convenience and also provided leads to early day railroaders.

James Gayner's loan of his valuable collection of CWR photographs was greatly appreciated.

A. E. Barker was most helpful in providing information on CWR locomotives as well as engineering data and manufacturer's drawings of the Skunk rail buses.

Richard Datin kindly produced his fine drawing of the Skunk for this book, and gave permission for use of his color photograph of the rail bus.

Appreciation is expressed to Hank Johnston, author of "Railroads of the Yosemite Valley," for a variety of suggestions; George Turner, author of "Slim Rails Through the Sand;" Linn Wescott, editor of Model Railroader Magazine; Woodbridge Metcalf, extension forester emeritus of the University of California, Berkeley; R. J. Pajalich, secretary of the California Public Utilities Commission; Jack Payne, the author's cousin and collector of Californiana; Del Jones, and Bill Pennington.

The author also expresses gratitude to B. J. Vaughn of The Union Lumber Company, Stuart Nixon of the Redwood Empire Association, J. G. Shea of the Southern Pacific, Randolph L. Kulp, and John T. Labbe.

Cathy Furniss, who so ably has publicized the CWR in recent years, also was helpful in preparing this edition.

Gratitude is offered to the Bancroft Library, the Public Library of the City and County of San Francisco, the library at the University of California Berkeley, the California Historical Society, the history room of the Wells Fargo Bank, the Oakland Public Library (and particularly its fine California Room so valuable to historians), the Fort Bragg Chamber of Commerce, the Willits Chamber of Commerce, and Mack Trucks, Inc.

And appreciation also is extended to John Galliani and King O. Nelson, engineer and conductor respectively aboard the Skunk on which the author rode during research for this book. The journey was memorable.

For additional reading in the area of redwoods and railroads, several books are recommended.

"Logging Railroads of the West" by Kramer Adams (Superior Publishing Company, Seattle: 1961) is a good general account of the subject indicated by the title.

"Redwood Classic" by Ralph W. Andrews (Superior Publishing Company, Seattle: 1958) is a presentation of the history of logging.

"The History of Mendocino and Lake Counties, California," by Aurelius O. Carpentier and Percy H. Millberry (Historic Record Company, Los Angeles: 1914) is a volume giving many details of the area's development.

"Redwood Railways" by Gilbert H. Kneiss (Howell-North Books, Berkeley: 1956) is an excellent account of efforts to build a railroad line northward from San Francisco.

"History of Mack Rail Motor Cars and Locomotives," edited by Randolph L. Kulp (Lehigh Valley Chapter, National Railway Historical Society, Inc., Allentown, Pennsylvania: 1959) is a detailed and interesting publication relative to rail buses.

"Railroads in the Woods" by John T. Labbe and Vernon Goe (Howell-North Books, Berkeley: 1961) is a fine volume with many illustrations depicting equipment.

"Trees of the Pacific Coast" by Howard E. McMinn and Evelyn Maino (University of California Press, Berkeley: 1937) contains information pertaining to the botany of redwoods.

"The History of Mendocino County" by Lyman Palmer (Bowen and Company, San Francisco: 1881) gives detailed accounts of early days in the redwoods.

"Redwood Country" by Alfred Powers (Duell, Sloan and Pearce, New York: 1949) is an excellent study of people and places as related to the redwoods.

"Memories of the Mendocino Coast" by David Warren Ryder (Taylor and Taylor, San Francisco: 1948) is a history of the Union Lumber Company.

SAN FRANCISCO

Spencer Crump

TABLE OF CONTENTS

The Appendix

Epilogue

1. *Skunk in the Redwoods*

Two visitors from Australia, making a hasty air trip to England, touched down in San Francisco. Although rushed, they paused to travel up the forested, wave-pounded coast of California to the city of Fort Bragg.

"We'd heard about the Skunk for years," the wife explained, "and we always would have regretted it, despite our haste, if we hadn't ridden it. We were quite willing to risk our reservations to Britain and wait for new ones if necessary.

"And the ride on the Skunk," she added with a smile, "was well worth the delay."

Not only the two Australians but visitors from throughout the United States and most sections of the world have eagerly made special trips to Fort Bragg, off the beaten path on the Mendocino Coast, for the unforgettable pleasure of riding the Skunk.

Approximately 40,000 people annually make the trek to Fort Bragg — a city of 5,000 residents some 150 miles north of San Francisco — for the explicit purpose of the two hour "Skunk" trip on rails through the redwood forests.

The Skunk is the name affectionately bestowed on the quaint rail buses operated for passengers on the California Western Railroad.

The CWR stretches from the Pacific Ocean at Fort Bragg through spectacular mountain country covered by magnificent redwoods, some so old they were growing before Jesus was born. Rolling over these tracks through tunnels and past verdant meadows, the Skunk rail buses carry passengers to the city of Willits.

Just who coined this most original title of "Skunk" given to the little rail buses evidently never was recorded. Nevertheless, the nickname long ago was taken to the hearts of rail fans, nature lovers, and

Steam locomotives reigned and pulled passenger coaches over the California Western's Redwood Route before the arrival of the "Skunk" rail buses.

a variety of others. The CWR even made "Skunk" the official designation for its passenger service.

The California Western Railroad Company is distinguished for a number of reasons.

It rates among the shortest railroads in the world, stretching only forty miles from the Pacific at Fort Bragg inland to Willits.

The Skunk's route is among the few where a resident may erect his own railroad station and be confident that the train will stop for passengers — or what's more, come to a halt even to receive a bystander signaling for a ride where there is no marked stop.

The rail line could boast that it had more bridges per mile (115 on completion and still 32 as late as 1963) than any other single railroad.

The line also is distinguished for its abundance of curves over its scenic route; the longest portion without curves stretches for less than a mile.

Its construction through the dense forest and steep mountains ranks among the most costly for each mile of any railroad in the world. Yet it was financed entirely by private capital without grants or public funds.

The California Western also is remarkable because it was scheduling additional passenger runs at the mid-point of the twentieth century, a time when other railroads, pressed by automobile and bus competition, were cutting service drastically.

While other railroads moaned the loss of passenger traffic, the CWR found it necessary to add to its roster of rolling equipment.

And the California Western was making its greatest strides to fame in the 1960's, long after the glory days of railroading had given the transcontinental lines a cherished niche in American tradition.

Helping the CWR to gain renown was its noted celebrity, the Skunk rail bus that was reminiscent both of the trolley car era and the days when the Iron Horse rolled and reigned supreme.

But the magnificence of the route it travels long ago earned the Skunk line eminence among railroads.

The peaks of the Coast Mountain range rise spectacularly, and the CWR right-of-way was hewn alongside the sparkling Noyo River, an attraction in itself. Covering the countryside are the majestic redwood trees, some higher than a thirty story building.

The fame of the California Western Railroad and its Skunk passenger cars has been of a latter-day nature. As the era of the steaming, puffing Iron Horse on its highway of steel rails vanished into the lore of early Americana, the CWR won acclaim for a variety of reasons.

Its scenic redwood setting, the heritage of the glory days of logging, the charm of its equipment, and the promise of its future commanded status and acclaim.

It is little wonder that 40,000 people annually travel from near and far, as did the pair from Australia, for the pleasant ride on the Skunk.

Part of the enchantment of a ride on the Skunk could be the proximity to nature presented as the rail bus glides around curves beneath the big trees that forgot to stop growing . . .

Perhaps much of the pleasure could be the cheerful smiles of the Skunk's crews, happily proclaiming that they themselves never tire of the journey . . .

Or quite possibly part of the fun is the fact that here is a railroad still serving, as it has for more than a half century, a useful purpose in surroundings unmarred by automobiles or airplanes.

Before we take a look at the California Western and its jovial but proud Skunk, let's go back and look at the redwood story itself.

It began many thousands of years ago . . .

The Mendocino Coast, rugged and beautiful, grew during the years as an attraction for visitors.

PHOTOGRAPH PAGE FOLLOWING:
REDWOOD EMPIRE ASSOCIATION

The beauty and grandeur of the redwood trees have always impressed men. Naturalist John Muir, who loved all trees, called the redwoods the "noblest of the noble."

The majestic trees are very old; in all probability they are the oldest living things in the world.

Botanists and other scientists are not positive when redwoods appeared on earth, but there is general agreement that the genus originated well over one hundred million years ago. Excavations of fossils indicate that redwoods covered large portions of the northern hemisphere during past geological ages. Most redwood forests vanished with climatic changes or when giant glaciers moved over vast areas of the earth, sweeping away trees as they changed the shapes of continents. Today redwoods are native only in two general portions of California, part of Oregon, and in limited numbers in one point in China.

Redwoods fall into the general botanical classification of *gymnospermae*, a group including all plants having seeds in open scales or cones. Within this grouping, the trees are classified in the *taxodiaceae* or redwood family. This group also includes such plants as the Chinese fir, umbrella pine, and bald cypress trees.[1]

More particularly, redwoods compose the genus botanists call *sequoia*, a name given in 1847 by an Austrian scholar, Stephen L. Endicher, while making a scholarly description of the spectacular trees. Endicher chose the name to honor the developer of the Cherokee alphabet, George Gist, whose Indian name was Sequoya.

California was blessed with not one but two varieties of redwoods. The *sequoia gigantea* species grow in the Sierra Nevada range and are most notable in Sequoia National Park. The other variety is the *sequoia sempervirens,* more popularly called the coastal redwoods. It is the latter trees that add beauty to the route of the California Western Railroad.

Both the coastal and inland redwood trees are distinguished for the reddish bark that logically inspired their name. Both varieties have simple, spirally arranged leaves and are always green.

The inland redwoods grow up to 300 feet tall and range up to 30 feet in diameter. Some individual trees

---

1. Howard E. McMinn and Evelyn Maino, "An Illustrated Manual of Pacific Coast Trees," Berkeley, 1947, Pp. 49-62. This volume provides botanical details of the redwoods and is an invaluable reference for other trees of the Pacific Coast.

The coastal redwoods dwarf men as they tower spectacularly and majestically, just as they have done for twenty centuries. Right, the Mendocino Coast.

are believed to be as old as four thousand years. These redwoods were veterans of a thousand years of life when the Greeks conquered Troy.

The coastal redwood trees are youngsters when compared to their inland cousins: the oldest of them are approximately 2,000 years old.

The coastal tree differs from the inland variety in that it grows taller — up to 340 feet or higher than a 35 story building. Its trunk is considerably slimmer, ranging up to 12 feet in diameter. The wood is not so fibrous as the inland redwood and is therefore stronger, making it more desirable for building.

The older and larger trees are the exception rather than the rule. Most of the trees are comparatively young, as redwoods are concerned, and range in age from saplings to veterans of several centuries.

Several other botanical details distinguish the two trees. The bark of the inland redwood is one to two feet thick, while the coastal cousin's bark ranges only up to twelve inches in thickness. Cones of the inland trees are two to three inches long while those of the coastal redwoods are considerably smaller, ranging up to one and a half inches long.

Actual size reproductions show how much larger are the cones of inland redwoods (above) than the coastal (below).

Botanists trace the differences to evidence that each type is a remnant of varying climatic and geological ages.

Tradition has it that the coastal redwoods were discovered when scavengers went northward from San Francisco during the gold rush era to salvage valuable silks aboard a Chinese ship wrecked on the treacherous coast near Cape Mendocino.

Actually the beauty and usefulness of the redwoods had been noted many years before — quite possibly as early as the Second Century, A. D.

An American missionary discovered documents in 1890 at the Chinese city of Si-Ngan-Foo that told of the discovery voyage. The reported journey to California took place in 217, A. D., aboard a junk captained by a seafarer named Hee-li.

This pre-Columbian trip to the land of the redwoods came as the result of a series of unfortunate incidences, according to the missionary's translation of the documents.[2]

Hee-li's junk blew to sea during a storm. When the waves subsided the vessel proceeded in the wrong direction. It seemed that a bug succumbed beneath the compass needle, causing it to point in the wrong direction. One seaman objected to the direction of the journey, basing his argument on the fact that direction of the sun's rising and setting had reversed.

Hee-li vested great faith in the compass, according to the missionary's translation, and therefore tossed the doubting crewman overboard and sailed onward. The junk eventually reached land at what is believed the present site of Monterey.

The Chinese spent three months exploring the area. Their hikes no doubt took them through the adjacent redwoods stretching in groves along the coast to southern Oregon.

The seamen returned to China, reporting the wrong-way voyage in documents translated by the missionary. The fact that Hee-li's account failed to mention the distinctive redwood trees possibly can be explained by the presence of similar trees at the time in China. Remnants of what were named the Dawn Redwoods were discovered in China during 1944. The trees may have grown there so abundantly when Hee-li made his unscheduled journey that he thought little of their presence in the new land.

It matters little whether Hee-Li's trek was fable or fact. There are records of other Oriental journeys to California in pre-Columbian times. Ships could travel along the coast of Asia, across the Bering Strait, and down the coast of North America without ever losing sight of land.

Undoubtedly these mariners stopped to admire the big redwood trees just as travelers would do in the centuries to come.

It seems dubious, however, that the European discoverer of California or his crew saw the redwoods. Juan Rodriguez Cabrillo, a Portuguese navigator sailing under the Spanish flag, discovered the area in 1542. Cabrillo died of injuries suffered while exploring the southern section. Accounts of his voyage indicate that the party made only limited explorations of the northern area.

The beauty of the redwoods certainly must have

2. New York Tribune, September 10, 1890. There are no records to indicate that scholars attempted to prove or disprove the veracity of the translation.

unfolded in 1579 for Sir Francis Drake, who claimed California for Queen Elizabeth I and named it Nova Albion (New England). To back up his claim, he left an inscribed brass plate—found in 1936 near Drake's Bay north of present day San Francisco. The location of the plate indicated he hardly could have missed the redwoods.

It was the Spanish who named the redwoods.

Pushing up the coast through the desert-like southern section of California in 1769, the Spanish explorers must have been refreshed to see the cacti and oak trees give way to the forests of lush trees near Monterey.

Father Juan Crespi, impressed with the bark of the trees, called them the *palo colorado*.

The name was translated to the English "redwood" and so it has remained.

The great forests of redwoods were forgotten for many years. Intent on securing settlements in the southern section, the Spanish built a series of missions, using the adobe so familiar to them in Mexico and other sections of Spanish America.

Had the mission chain continued northward as projected, it would have extended into the redwood country north of San Francisco Bay. There the great rainfall would have forced the Spanish to abandon adobe and utilize the more durable redwood for construction.

Russians, rather than the Spanish or Americans, were probably the first to rely on redwood for extensive housing needs.

The Czar chartered the Russian American Company with powers similar to those the British crown granted to the Hudson's Bay Company and the East India Company. The Russians, hunting and selling valuable furs, first were active in Alaska and then began to move southward. As early as 1803 Russian hunters were reported along the coast of California. By 1841 the Russians were entrenching themselves in the area. Duflot de Mofras, a Frenchman, toured the Pacific Coast and was quoted by historian Hubert Bancroft as reporting:

The (Russian) company realizes immense profits from this branch of commerce. The Kodiaks, in their canoes of seal skins, make fierce war on the sea wolves, or beaver, and above all on the sea-otter; they exploit the entire coast, the neighboring islands, the Farollones, and even the innumerable marshes and canals of the port of San Francisco. There are weeks in which this bay alone produces seven or eight hundred otter skins.

17

The Russians established a base in 1812 on Bodega Bay, north of San Francisco and just south of the site to become Fort Bragg.

The settlement was named Fort Ross (based on a root of "Russia"). High on a plateau by the ocean, the Russians built a stockade and warehouse.

The Russians used redwood for the construction.

So durable was the redwood, its tough fiber weathering the salt air, rain, and years, that, unattended, the fort stood. When well past its century mark, Fort Ross was preserved as a state historical monument.

The Russian's presence brought a distinctively negative reaction from the Spanish and their successors after the revolution, the Mexicans. In 1842 Mariano Vallejo, governor of California, bluntly suggested that they sell their redwood installation and depart for their homeland. They accepted the warning. The purchaser of the property was Captain John Sutter, a Swiss adventurer.

Gold discovered on Sutter's property on the American River near Sacramento in 1848 started the famous gold rush that brought settlers and subsequently statehood to California.

Quite appropriately, and somewhat poetically, the wreck of a Chinese ship reminiscent of Hee-li's voyage brought the value and beauty of the redwoods to the attention of the Americans. The men who went northward to salvage the silk returned with glowing descriptions of the stately big trees.

Others quickly went northward, carrying equipment to down the trees and mill them into lumber to help build San Francisco.

The arrival of these Americans was not welcomed by the area's Indians, who had heard how settlers decimated tribes in other sections. They attacked the loggers.

A cry for military aid brought First Lieutenant Horatio G. Gibson from the presidio of San Francisco. North of the Noyo River (named for the Noyo

An artist made this sketch of Fort Ross shortly after it was built — mostly of redwood — by the Russians.

This 1862 sketch depicts Fort Bragg when activities at the coastal military post were hitting a peak.

Indian tribe) he established a stockade at an inlet call Soldiers Harbor.

The lieutenant named the installation Fort Bragg, honoring Captain Braxton Bragg, a West Point classmate whom he greatly admired. Captain Bragg never had the pleasure of visiting California and seeing the place named in his honor. When the Civil War started, he resigned his army position and joined the Confederate Army as a major general. Bragg received a painting of the outpost, but this treasure was destroyed when advancing Union forces burned his plantation.

The Indians, less warlike following the arrival of Lieutenant Gibson's detachment, soon retired to a reservation. Fort Bragg was abandoned in 1867.

Before its abandonment, Fort Bragg was singled out as a beauty spot of the coast. A Ukiah writer in 1863 sung these praises:[3]

We will now transport the reader to the most lovely location in the county — Fort Bragg. This port is situated one and one half miles north of the Noyo river, upon the government reservation. It is not anything like a fortification, but is the nicest little village we have ever seen. There would seem to have been a provision of nature, that this coast shall at least have one beautiful spot upon it. Fort Bragg is merely a smooth, sloping open piece of ground in a pine forest, with the various buildings encircling the open space, which is about ten acres in extent. The slope of the ground is towards the ocean, from whose biting winds it is sheltered by a thick belt of pines . . . The buildings are comfortable and neat, inside and out, and all painted and white-washed.

Seventeen years later, however, the picture had changed. After inspecting the site in 1880, a contemporary writer sadly reported:[4]

But how changed are all things now! The reservation was abandoned in 1867, and the military post was no longer needed nor sustained, and from that time on everything has been allowed to go to decay and ruin. Long years ago the paint and white-wash had been washed off from the buildings by the fogs of summer and the rains of winter, and their places have been taken by a boat of green moss. The fence that was once the pride of the commandant has gone to wreck along with everything else, and now the public highway bisects the parade ground.

Soon after the fort's abandonment, the land was offered for $1.25 an acre to settlers. Even this bargain price failed to revive the area.

Fort Bragg might have been little more than a memory, marked only by a legend on old maps, had it not been for the imagination and ability of a young man named Charles Russell Johnson.

3. Palmer, Lyman L., "History of Mendocino County," San Francisco, 1880, Pp. 428-30. The author quoted from a newspaper clipping describing Fort Bragg.

4. Palmer, Lyman L., "History of Mendocino County," San Francisco, 1880, P. 430.

*Loggers called time out while downing this big red-
wood tree during the mid-nineteenth century for this
picture. Twelve people, including two young women,
were able to perch in the undercut of the tree.*

Here is the way San Francisco looked in 1873 when C. R. Johnson first visited the city, rapidly becoming one of the west's great business and cultural centers.

3. The Young Man from Wisconsin

Gold and silver from the mines of California's Mother Lode and Nevada's Comstock Lode built San Francisco. In turn, the City by the Golden Gate built itself with lumber from the redwood forests.

Once downed by the loggers, the big redwoods usually reached San Francisco via the sea. Sometimes the timber went by ship, but in many cases the rough logs were tied together and floated, like a big raft, to the Golden Gate.

The redwood timber went into the great buildings that helped make San Francisco both the cultural and financial center of a major part of the American West. Its sphere encompassed not only California, Nevada, Washington, and Oregon but also Alaska, purchased in 1867 from Russia for the bargain price of $7.2 million.

The Central Pacific's steel rails linked California to America's eastern seaboard less than twenty years

Here is the way Fort Ross looked in 1877, more than a half century after being built. The durable redwood stood up well against the salt air and rains.

after statehood in 1850. Tides of excited settlers arrived expectantly by the trainload. Each day brought news of mining discoveries and commercial development. San Francisco, hub of activity, took its place as a cosmopolitan city of culture, beauty, and commerce unequaled on the Pacific Coast. The state teemed with prosperity and excitement.

Into this atmosphere arrived Charles Russell Johnson. He was born at Racine, Wisconsin, on St. Valentine's Day in 1859. While he was a boy, his family moved to Michigan. There his father operated

sawmills at Saugatuck and St. Ignace. This environment would shape the youth's destiny as well as that of the redwood industry.

The youth had a bout with illness that prompted his father to send him west to recuperate. So it was that 14-year-old Charles Johnson arrived in San Francisco in 1873.

He soon recovered his health, visited in the area for eighteen months, and then returned to work in his father's mill. After two years he left to take a job with the Menominee River Lumber Company in Chicago. There he worked for four years, absorbing

Oxen pull redwood logs down an incline in this picture of early day activities near Fort Bragg. Such primitive methods soon yielded to locomotives.

23

many details relative to production techniques, marketing methods, and uses for lumber.

The visit to California had impressed young Johnson. In 1881, when twenty-three years old, he returned to the Pacific Coast to make it his home.

The youth traveled extensively in California, but failed to find what he wanted.

One day he visited a family friend, A. B. Starr, founder of the Starr Flour Mills at Crockett. Starr spoke in glowing terms of the big redwoods north of San Francisco. Young Johnson persuaded him to accompany him to see the trees.

A tedious, difficult journey carried them northward. The trip was via railroad and then by buckboard stage. Hired team and wagon over barely discernible roads took them on the last leg of the trek.

When Charles Russell Johnson saw the stately redwoods of the Mendocino Coast, he knew why he decided to make California his home.

He fell in love with the redwoods with an affection that was to continue until his death nearly sixty years later.

Men with other backgrounds might merely have marvelled at the great trees. Young Johnson certainly gazed in awe at the redwoods, but his lumber background enabled him to see their potential in a deeper vein. He decided to enter the redwood business.

Among those he met during the journey were Calvin Stewart and James Hunter, veteran loggers in the area north of abandoned Fort Bragg. Young Johnson purchased an interest in their holdings. The firm of Stewart, Hunter, and Johnson was born.

"C. R.," as the youth was dubbed, promptly proved his worth as a partner by introducing innovations that revolutionized redwood logging.

Johnson bought modern machinery he had noted in the midwest, and the partners' logging operations became more efficient. Mills traditionally worked a

A gasoline saw helps loggers in crosscutting a downed redwood that will be hauled to the Fort Bragg mills.

Cross Cutting
Mile Camps

24

single shift; Johnson put operations on a twenty-four hour basis. The output more than doubled.

Logging methods of the era were crude by modern standards. After being downed by handsaws and axes, hand-operated devices moved the trees. Oxen hauled the logs to rivers to be floated to mills. Moreover, the treacherous sea and lack of harbors along the Mendocino coast made it difficult for sizeable vessels to serve the mills. Getting the lumber to San Francisco was vital to the economics of the redwood industry.

Operations of the Stewart, Hunter, and Johnson partnership centered on Mill Creek, a tributary of the Ten Mile River north of Fort Bragg. The closest shipping point was Newport, reached only after hauling lumber for nearly ten miles by horse and wagon.

Only the smallest lumber schooners could anchor at Newport, and then only after waiting for a favorable tide permitting them to maneuver under a lumber chute descending from a bluff. Up to a week was required for loading a single small schooner.

"C. R." combed the area for a more advantageous loading point. The search narrowed to the abandoned army post of Fort Bragg. Alongside the decaying buildings was Soldiers Harbor, a sheltered cove large enough for sizable ships.

Johnson envisioned more than a mere shipping point: he foresaw a city established along with a major mill. Substantial capital would be needed.

He organized the Fort Bragg Lumber Company, and those who purchased stock included his father, Otis R. Johnson, as well as two friends in Michigan.

The new organization purchased the assets of Stewart, Hunter, and Johnson, along with additional timber properties owned by the firm of McPherson and Weatherby on Pudding Creek, the Noyo River, and the site of Fort Bragg itself.

The first step was building a wharf to receive equipment as well as to ship lumber once operations started. A mill then was constructed.

At ten o'clock on the morning of November 16, 1885, Johnson started a bandsaw — a new invention purchased by the new firm.

The Fort Bragg Lumber Company, forerunner of one of America's great redwood organizations, was in business.

Not content with founding the lumber company, "C. R." proceeded to start the city of Fort Bragg. When the municipality was incorporated in 1889,

Charles R. Johnson introduced improved logging methods and started the California Western Railroad.

citizens selected him for the honor of being the first mayor.

The use of a bandsaw to speed milling operations was not to be the only innovation.

Eager to use all available machinery of the era, Johnson eyed the steel rails and Iron Horses of the railroads.

These "tracks" of timber were used by oxen pulling cars loaded with logs during early lumber operations. Locomotives make logging more efficient and easier.

4. *Iron Horse in the Redwoods*

Railroads, at least of a primitive nature, made their debut as early as 1852 in the California redwoods. Mules and oxen generally pulled log cars over rails, shaped from lumber in many instances. Completion of the Central Pacific inspired numerous logging companies to purchase steam locomotives to speed operations.

In most operations, rails were laid and lifted according to logging needs of the moment. There was little, if any, effort to maintain regular schedules or to encourage passenger traffic. Logging railroads basically were transient, operating when needed and moved to reach the supply of trees.[1]

The railroad founded by C. R. Johnson became an entirely different type of line. It played an important part not only in the area's industrial life, but also in its social and cultural activities.

No other logging railroads on the Pacific Coast made the deep impression on American life that was created by the line from Fort Bragg — first by the beauty of its route and later by distinctiveness of equipment.

The name chosen for the line was, appropriately, The Fort Bragg Railroad. The articles of incorporation filed April 30, 1885, reflected a somewhat less ambitious undertaking than the railroad and its successor came to be.

(See Appendix for the articles of incorporation for the Fort Bragg Railroad Company.)

The articles provided for a 20-mile line from Fort Bragg up the Noyo River plus a branch to the Ten Mile River.

Options for construction of narrow gauge (3'6") or standard gauge (4'8½") tracks were allowed in the documents.

By the time the first track was laid later in 1885, Johnson and his fellow lumbermen had decided on a standard gauge railroad. This decision no doubt

---

1. Several books deal with the operation of logging railroads. An excellent general discussion is found in "Logging Railroads of the West" by Kramer A. Adams (Superior Publishing Company, Seattle). "Railroads in the Woods" by John T. Labbe and Vernon Goe (Howell-North Books, Berkeley) emphasizes equipment. Both books are profusely illustrated.

was based on considerations that standard rail equipment could be utilized and rolling stock could interchange, if connections eventually were made, with the transcontinental roads.

Johnson and his associates evidently regarded the railroad with growing enthusiasm as an economic necessity to replace the slow operations of mules and oxen.

The first track stretched from the shores of the Pacific at Soldiers Harbor up Pudding Creek toward the redwoods earmarked for mill operations.

The initial locomotive acquired was appropriately named *Sequoia*. Its arrival by ship at Fort Bragg in 1886 was greeted by curiosity, wonderment, and cheers.

The *Sequoia* was built by the Baldwin Locomotive Works, rated among America's leading producers of railway rolling stock. The importance of the rail line to the lumber company as well as intentions to develop the system into something more than the usual logging operation may be noted in the selection of equipment. Most contemporary logging companies were content to utilize second hand or inferior rail equipment if adequate to haul logs to a loading or milling point.

The *Sequoia,* also known as No. 1 for its numerical designation, was small by transcontinental standards of the day but was certainly substantial for the service intended. Its weight was 56,000 pounds. Engines used at the time for transcontinental service averaged 85,000 pounds.

Pushing the tracks up Pudding Creek was coupled with logging operations on adjoining timberland. The line was helping to pay its way as it was built. Logs went by rail down to Fort Bragg to be milled and shipped as finished lumber from Soldiers Harbor.

The new railroad got some what of a running start in its construction by absorbing the Pudding Creek Railroad Company, started in 1881 by McPherson and Weatherby and acquired by the Fort Bragg Lumber Company in purchasing the former firm.

By 1887 the Fort Bragg Railroad stretched 6.6 miles up Pudding Creek, reaching a point designated as Glen Blair. Here the Glen Blair Lumber Company sent its shipments of redwood to be carried by rail to Fort Bragg, providing the railway company with revenue in addition to that from its parent firm.

This year also saw the Fort Bragg Railroad purchasing its second locomotive. No. 2, also built by

Log pilings for a mighty trestle are driven as part of the construction stretching the railway from Fort Bragg to the interior. Timber was plentiful for building, but the rugged country called for skilled engineering and heavy physical energy.

the Baldwin Locomotive Works, but slightly larger than its working mate, weighed 62,000 pounds.

The railroad already was finding a special place in the hearts of Fort Bragg residents. A San Francisco streetcar was purchased and converted for use as a passenger coach. It carried jovial parties of log-

27

These visitors rode the Iron Horse from Fort Bragg to see the much discussed "end of the tracks" in the early twentieth century.

gers, with their girl friends or wives, on Sunday picnic outings along Pudding Creek.

Despite long days at work in the forests, the loggers enjoyed the beauty and tranquility of the redwoods for recreation.

Operations were expanding and more capital was needed. The vehicle for this expansion was the Union Lumber Company, the articles of incorporation for which were filed August 17, 1893. The new corporation assumed not only the assets of the Fort Bragg Redwood Company but also of White and Plummer, a firm owning large timber tracts in the area.

Plans included taking timber standing near the Noyo River, separated by a mountain slope from Pudding Creek. Most important, the mountain was a barrier to the railroad, effective for logging.

A tunnel would be the best way to reach the proposed logging area, but it seemed few men wanted the work of tunneling through the rocky slope. Excavating lacked the appeal of open air work in the redwoods.

"C. R." put in a call for Chinese laborers, experienced as tunnel builders since their days on the

Central Pacific construction through the Sierra Nevada range.

Rabid resentment against the Chinese had developed as a California tradition because of their willingness to work for less money than other men. Hatred, abuse, and physical violence marked relations with the Chinese throughout the state.

The arrival of the Chinese in Fort Bragg brought forth an outbreak of bigotry in the tranquil redwoods. White men, resenting the mere appearance of Chinese, rallied and began a campaign of abuse designed to frighten the Orientals away.

Tempers flared and it appeared there would be bloodshed. However, a cool-minded law officer stepped forward with some most logical arguments.

Mendocino County Sheriff William Standley (and the father of Admiral W. H. Standley, World War II ambassador to Russia) approached the trouble makers.

"How many of you are willing," he asked, "to volunteer to dig this tunnel?"

The men, mulling over such a distasteful proposal as digging a tunnel, were silent to a man.

"Very well," the sheriff was quoted as saying, "it is just as I suspected. You men are not willing to do

CALIFORNIA WESTERN RAILROAD COLLECTION

These railway construction workers paused for a picture alongside a pile of ties while pushing rails into the mountains.

this hard and dangerous work and for that I'm not blaming you.

"But in that case, you certainly should not prevent these Chinamen from doing it.

"Now I know you are fair-minded men," Standley continued, showing good psychology and probably observing many in the crowd straighten with pride, "so I suggest you disperse and go home so that these China boys who know how to do this work can go back to work."

The men took the sheriff's suggestion and left the Chinese to blast and dig.

The tunnel — 1,122 feet long — was completed in 1893. Tracks stretched through it from Pudding Creek to the Noyo River, opening up new territory for economical logging and breaking the railroad's first major barrier toward inland connections.

Disaster in form of a business depression struck in 1893. Lumber prices slumped and so did work on the railroad, since logging was its basic purpose for existing as well as the source for financing. The mill continued to run, although at a slower pace. Equally

Downed by logging crews, these redwoods will be hauled to a mill for finishing into lumber.

UNIVERSITY OF CALIFORNIA
SCHOOL OF FORESTRY

slowly, the tracks stretched up the Noyo River as timber was cut.

By 1898 the tracks reached approximately 10 miles past Fort Bragg to the Little North Fork of the Noyo River. The train carried passengers bound for San Francisco to this point; from there they rode a buckboard stage to Willits, where connection was made for another stagecoach reaching the railroad at Ukiah.

The stage trip was an ordeal financially as well as physically. The stagecoach fair was $8.50 between Fort Bragg and Ukiah, constituting less than a third of the total mileage to San Francisco. The rail fare from Ukiah to San Francisco was much more reasonably priced — as well as more comfortable — and cost just $4.50.

Railroads were a generally popular preoccupation with the early twentieth century American public, just as apparatus for travel into space was to capture imaginations sixty years later. Spectacular displays of big and ornate trains at the 1893 World Columbian Exposition in Chicago kindled a great fascination over trains that burned for years. Crack passenger trains were going into service throughout the nation, and new speculation developed daily over proposed rail lines.

The presence of a railroad signaled growth for a community that otherwise would have been doomed to obscurity. The Iron Horse opened new vistas in isolated towns, carrying residents quickly and relatively safely to the romanticized metropolitan centers.

Much of a community's activities centered around the railroad depot, where townspeople traditionally gathered during idle hours to survey newcomers arriving on the train.

Residents of every city rated a railroad as a status symbol, and the people of Fort Bragg were no exception.

Fort Bragg residents yearned for rail connections to San Francisco, the shopping, business, and cultural center of the Pacific Coast. They visualized not only the pleasant trip from Fort Bragg in a rail car, but they also expected thousands from the bay area either to make the trip for sightseeing among the great red-

A locomotive steams past an area where track construction was under way. Note how the trees had been logged, thanks to the convenience of the railroad.

CALIFORNIA WESTERN RAILROAD

Time out from track construction was called so these workers could pose for a picture of early building activities. Eager to be on with the important job, however, one laborer (left) continued with his duties with such energy that his image was blurred.

The abundant timber in the mountains proved useful in constructing the railroad. This picture of early day building shows logs forming a support for the right-of-way hugging a mountain.

woods or to migrate to settle permanently for the pleasant life in the forests.

Each new mile of track was gratefully noted and saluted by residents of Fort Bragg. Some had their doubts regarding the curving and difficult route cut up the canyon of the Noyo River.

"Locomotive No. 1 has made several trips up Cannon Ball Gulch lately," the Fort Bragg Advocate reported after an 1899 extension. "Mrs. Fred Severance is the first lady to ride over this piece of road. She had good nerve."[2]

As citizens watched the progress of the Fort Bragg Railroad, they also eyed the news of the projected rail lines that would connect San Francisco with Eureka and, subsequently, Seattle. Independent railroad companies slowly laid track northward from San Francisco, but it was obvious that substantial money would be required for the big push over the rugged mountain terrain south of Eureka. Competing rail lines reportedly were planned by E. H. Harriman, president of the Southern Pacific, and E. P. Ripley, head of the Santa Fe. Each vowed that nothing could stop the competition except the other stepping aside.[3]

This competition, as expensive as it might be to the big companies paying the bills, was quite welcome to Fort Bragg and other towns along the way that wanted the vital rail links for passengers and freight.

C. R. Johnson and his associates in the Union Lumber Company eagerly sought to oblige as far as the connection from Fort Bragg was concerned. The rails from Fort Bragg were going through the redwoods and over the mountains so that the tracks could inter-change with those of the transcontinental lines when they arrived.

Construction was tedious and difficult from Fort Bragg. Tracks necessarily crossed and re-crossed the Noyo River as the right-of-way was carved from the mountains. Many bridges spanned the river.

These bridges varied from those on other railroads. While other lines could sink supporting timbers in the river beds, the Fort Bragg Railroad could do no such thing because of the danger from floating logs. Instead, "A" frame bridges — so named because the stress was carried on beams atop the structure — were erected to avoid impediment from debris.[4]

The rainfall, approaching 50 inches annually, not only slowed construction but also frequently brought floods that washed out track sections and bridges. Rains also brought landslides, covering tracks and suddenly blocking or even derailing engines that rounded curves hiding the debris.

In 1904 the tracks reached Alpine, 18.1 miles from Fort Bragg. The Alpine Tavern was constructed, soon becoming popular as a tourist resort as well as the station for boarding the buckboard stage for the next lap of the trip to San Francisco.

Leaving the Fort Bragg Railroad at Alpine, passengers rode the stage to Sherwood, a few miles north of Willits. At Sherwood they boarded the independently owned California Northwestern Railroad for Ukiah and then on to Sausalito, the point for ferries to San Francisco.

It was to be several years before the dream of the Iron Horse from the Pacific climbing the hill to Willits became a reality, but the legal machinery to make the line a reality soon was to be created.

The spirit for the big jump through the mountains already was very much alive.

---

4. The picturesque "A" frame bridges gradually were replaced by more substantial steel structures. The last remaining "A" frame bridge was doomed for replacement in 1963.

The Union Lumber Company made these houses available to employees and their families for the bargain rental of $2.50 monthly during the early twentieth century.

---

2. Fort Bragg Advocate, September 25, 1899.

3. A dramatic study of rail construction northward from San Francisco is presented in "Redwood Railways" (Berkeley, 1956) by Gilbert H. Kneiss.

These loggers stopped for lunch alongside the rail-road tracks after downing trees to be picked up later in the day by a train for hauling to Fort Bragg.

This rail car rolled merrily past a redwood fringed meadow enroute to Fort Bragg. Seated with the adults are two children, indicating that even in this early day the railroad provided an attraction for youngsters.

CALIFORNIA WESTERN RAILROAD COLLECTION

Locomotive No. 4, purchased in 1904, had just been put into service when its crew members posed with loggers after picking up a shipment of timber.

5. A New Railroad Is Born

The early twentieth century found the Union Lumber Company taking its place among the major logging organizations of the Pacific Coast. Or, as C. R. Johnson put it in his memoirs, the company was "out of the woods and picking up right along."

The company was very much in the redwoods, however, and going deeper — thanks to the Fort Bragg Railroad. The Iron Horse faithfully followed the rails into the forests. It hauled logs to Fort Bragg for milling and subsequent shipment as finished lumber on steamers from Soldiers Harbor.

Completion of the line through the mountains to Willits remained a dream, as did the projected rival

Southern Pacific and Santa Fe routes linking San Francisco, Eureka, and points northward.

The continued reliance on the Pacific Ocean for shipping was demonstrated when representatives of the Union Lumber Company incorporated the National Steamship Company on June 24, 1901. The new firm's ships carried lumber from other mills as well as for its parent company. A welcome aboard sounded for passengers, too. Many travelers preferred the relaxing ocean voyage instead of the stagecoach trip over the rough mountain terrain.

Control of the shipping company rather than reliance on individual vessels also assured regular

35

Conquering the mighty mountains, a steam shovel moves dirt (above) to make way for the railroad tracks from Fort Bragg. Laborers clear a slide (below) as they lay rails through the mountains.

CALIFORNIA WESTERN RAILROAD COLLECTION

Locomotive No. 5 pulls a cargo of redwood logs to the wharf at Fort Bragg. Many of the logs were shipped or floated to San Francisco for milling.

schedules for bringing merchandise to Fort Bragg shops, including Union's own public department store.

The firm's first vessel was the *Brunswick,* a 512-ton steamship purchased in 1903. Early in 1906 the company acquired the *National City,* a 310-ton steam vessel built eighteen years earlier in San Francisco.

Even the steamship company did not mean an end for the picturesque shipping of unfinished logs by floating in the open sea. Logs tied with immense chains formed cigar-shaped rafts containing up to five million log feet of lumber. "Mother" ships served as tows to float the big rafts to San Francisco.

While the locomotives' primary work duty called for bringing logs from the forests, the Fort Bragg Railroad soon departed from the "all freight" function of most logging lines. Regular daily passenger service to Alpine started in 1904 with completion of this extension. The existing Sunday excursions into the redwoods remained a popular "extra" service for the Iron Horse.

A high-climber starts up a redwood tree to begin work during an early day logging operation.

The year 1905 was to be a time of growth for both the Union Lumber Company and its railroad operations.

The new legal entity selected for rail expansion was the California-Western Railroad and Navigation Company, incorporated June 30, 1905 by the lumber firm's representatives.[1]

(See Appendix for the articles of incorporation of the California-Western Railroad and Navigation Company.)

Founding directors were listed as Charles H. Weller, an auditor for Union; Max Goldberg, president of the San Francisco Collateral Loan Bank; Duncan McNee, secretary of the bank; H. M. Cochran, Union's San Francisco yard manager, and Miles W. McIntosh, a San Francisco attorney.

The incorporation documents listed W. P. Plummer, Union director and stockholder, as subscribing to 625 shares of the new company. Each of the five railroad company directors held five shares of stock to qualify for places on the board.

Plummer, of course, was listed as holding the bulk of the stock because he was serving as trustee for his employer, the Union Lumber Company.

The articles of incorporation outlined the proposed trackage, including a main line to Willits over a route of 41 miles (which proved to be just 40 miles when eventually completed).

The document estimated that the new company eventually would construct main and branch lines with a total of 65 miles; when at its peak during the 1920's, the railroad had slightly over 50 miles of track.

Indicating the potential envisioned for the primitive area, the by-laws provided that the new company could conduct pleasure resorts and extend its tracks to towns expected to mushroom in the forests.

Just how the name "California Western" was selected for the company seems to have been lost in the pages of time.

On July 1, the day after its official incorporation, the new firm assumed operation of what had been the Fort Bragg Railroad. The task of winding the tracks into the redwood forests started.

---

1. The company's name officially was hyphenated "California-Western." The railroad popularly was called the "California Western" even before the hyphen was dropped effective January 1, 1948, when the "and Navigation" officially was removed from the corporate name. The firm itself never operated ships.

Locomotive No. 8 stops in the redwoods during a trip in about 1910. Trainmen included engineer Ed Hendrickson, conductor Arthur Hanson, and brakeman John Pimentel, all of whom eventually served on the first passenger train from Fort Bragg to Willits.

After riding to the point where the CWR tracks end-ed in about 1907, these travelers boarded a stage-coach for the next leg of the trip to San Francisco.

McIntosh, an attorney, became the CWR's first president and Weller was named treasurer.

More expansion for Union came on December 30 when it purchased the controlling interest in the Mendocino Lumber Company, owning redwood forests at the nearby town of Mendocino. Union in 1905 also acquired a fifty per cent interest in the Glen Blair Lumber Company, operating north of Pudding Creek.

Fort Bragg residents were intensely interested in the battle between the Southern Pacific and Santa Fe over parallel routes between Eureka and San Francisco. The city's newspaper, the Fort Bragg Advocate, ran frequent articles detailing the battle between giants.

The townspeople hoped that the California Western would reach Willits in time to connect with whichever major line first reached there from San Francisco.

Speculation over rail construction abruptly halted, at least temporarily, when disaster struck Fort Bragg in the spring of 1906. The California Western as well

Hugging the Noyo River, the California Western tracks are pushed deeper into the rugged interior region as the line moves to its eventual terminus.

as the National Steamship Company played important parts in reducing effects of the tragedy.

The memorable date was April 18. The earthquake that shook San Francisco and contributed to fires that destroyed major portions of the city also jolted the quiet little town of Fort Bragg.

Buildings in Fort Bragg's downtown area tumbled and fires started.

The jolt broke water pipes, making it almost impossible to fight the flames.

The earthquake tilted the Union Lumber Company's mill building twenty degrees. Smokestacks atop the structure tilted as though they were toys tipped by a child's hand. Fires were beginning to spread in the mill area, which with its dry lumber would burn like a tinder box.[2]

It seemed as though the broken water pipes would bring the same tragedy that at the very moment was razing San Francisco. For Fort Bragg this fate would be more tragic, at least proportionately, since virtually everyone in town directly or indirectly depended on the lumber mill for livelihoods.

Desperate residents mourned that there was ample water at Pudding Creek but no way to use it with the pipes broken.

_____

2. Fort Bragg Advocate, April 25, 1906.

Fortunately for Fort Bragg, C. R. Johnson was on hand with his railroad and steamship.

Mr. Johnson described the quick action in his memoirs:

> Luckily there was a locomotive under steam, so we hastily summoned it and ran it down the track, which at the time was laid on the pond dam, and so got the locomotive close to the power house. By this time there was a big crowd of men around the mill and they connected the locomotive boiler with the fire pump which could get water from the mill pond. We did this in remarkably quick time and by pouring water into the furnaces put out their fires and removed all danger from the mill.

> Meanwhile, the company's steamer, *National City*, moved to the mill and its crew gathered hose that was stretched up to the city to extinguish fire on the burning buildings.

The townspeople were more gratified than ever because they had a railroad and steamship line. Although San Francisco burned, most of Fort Bragg was saved — thanks to the motive power.

Even so, the aftermath of the earthquake found Fort Bragg counting one fatality: a merchant identified as "Le Poie." The community reckoned its damage at nearly a million dollars.

After the fires were controlled, C. R. Johnson boarded the *National City* for a quick trip to suffering San Francisco. The steamer was a welcome aid in helping evacuate the injured to Oakland, damaged itself but still in better condition to receive the victims.

The *National City* loaded supplies in the bay area to help rebuild Fort Bragg. Johnson not only let those without funds as a result of the earthquake "pay later" in the Union department store but also extended credit to competing merchants so they could restock and remain in business.

When the Fort Bragg Advocate reported details of the earthquake in its April 25 edition, it praised Union's role:

> With their usual liberality and encouragement, the Union Lumber Company are doing the right thing by the people and Fort Bragg will arise from her ashes and ruins a better and more substantial town.

The newspaper's references to Union as "their" instead of the gramatically correct "its" was typical of early day references. The public was beginning to look on the company as a collection of people instead of the inanimate object it legally was.

This train of cars carrying giant redwood logs was typical of traffic on the California Western. The logs were taken to Fort Bragg for milling into lumber.

The post-earthquake period brought prosperity to Fort Bragg. The mills hummed with activity as San Francisco purchased lumber to rebuild. Speculation resumed over the proposed railroad routes into the redwoods.

Troubles were not over for Fort Bragg. The winter of 1906-07 brought heavy rains. Downpours hindered logging, and what was worse for extended rail connections, floods wiped out immense sections of the California Western tracks.

Crews were dispatched immediately to repair the right-of-way, but it took three months of hard work in the mud and steep slopes to get the Iron Horse operating again to Alpine.

Perhaps the CWR's tremendous expenses of building and maintenance in the mountainous redwood country frightened the Southern Pacific and Santa Fe over high costs of pushing competing lines through similar terrain to reach Eureka and connect with Seattle. It was obvious that a sparsely populated region contributing mainly logging shipments could not support two railroads built at such immense costs.

As powerful and stubborn as were the tycoons controlling the two major railroads, they had no desire to test their strength in a battle in the redwoods. Late in 1906 the Southern Pacific and Santa Fe

Train Load Of Logs For Union Lumber Co.s Mill, Fort Bragg, Cal.

CALIFORNIA WESTERN RAILROAD

ER TRAIN IN FORT BRAGG WOODS.

Photo.

Logs for milling and other freight are carried on the CWR tracks stretching into the redwood forest.

$50 REWARD!

A reward of Fifty Dollars ($50.00) will be paid for information leading to the arrest and conviction of any person, or persons, maliciously destroying or damaging property of this Company.

CALIFORNIA WESTERN R. R. & NAV. COMPANY

This notice was posted by the railroad along the tracks to discourage vandals. Right, members of a rail inspection crew stopped their car to pose for a picture by a big tree.

reached a compromise opening the way for the long anticipated rail route north of San Francisco. The two giants formed the jointly owned Northwestern Pacific Railroad to build and operate the line.

Completion of the route to Willits and then northward loomed imminent. Work started, but came to a halt under the pressure of the Depression of 1907. Not until 1909 was work resumed, and progress then was slow because of high construction costs through the mountainous terrain.

Despite the sad news from the Northwestern Pacific, 1908 brought a happy word for California Western passengers. The line purchased two passen-

ger coaches to replace the converted streetcar. A combination coach and baggage car was numbered "42," while the exclusively passenger car was given the nuber "43."

Meanwhile, the CWR was purchasing new and larger locomotives to serve its passenger and logging schedules.

(See Appendix for the roster of locomotives used by the Fort Bragg and California Western Railroads.)

The CWR tracks slowly wound their way through the redwoods toward Willits. Logging camps opened and the Iron Horse carried loggers to work. Passen-

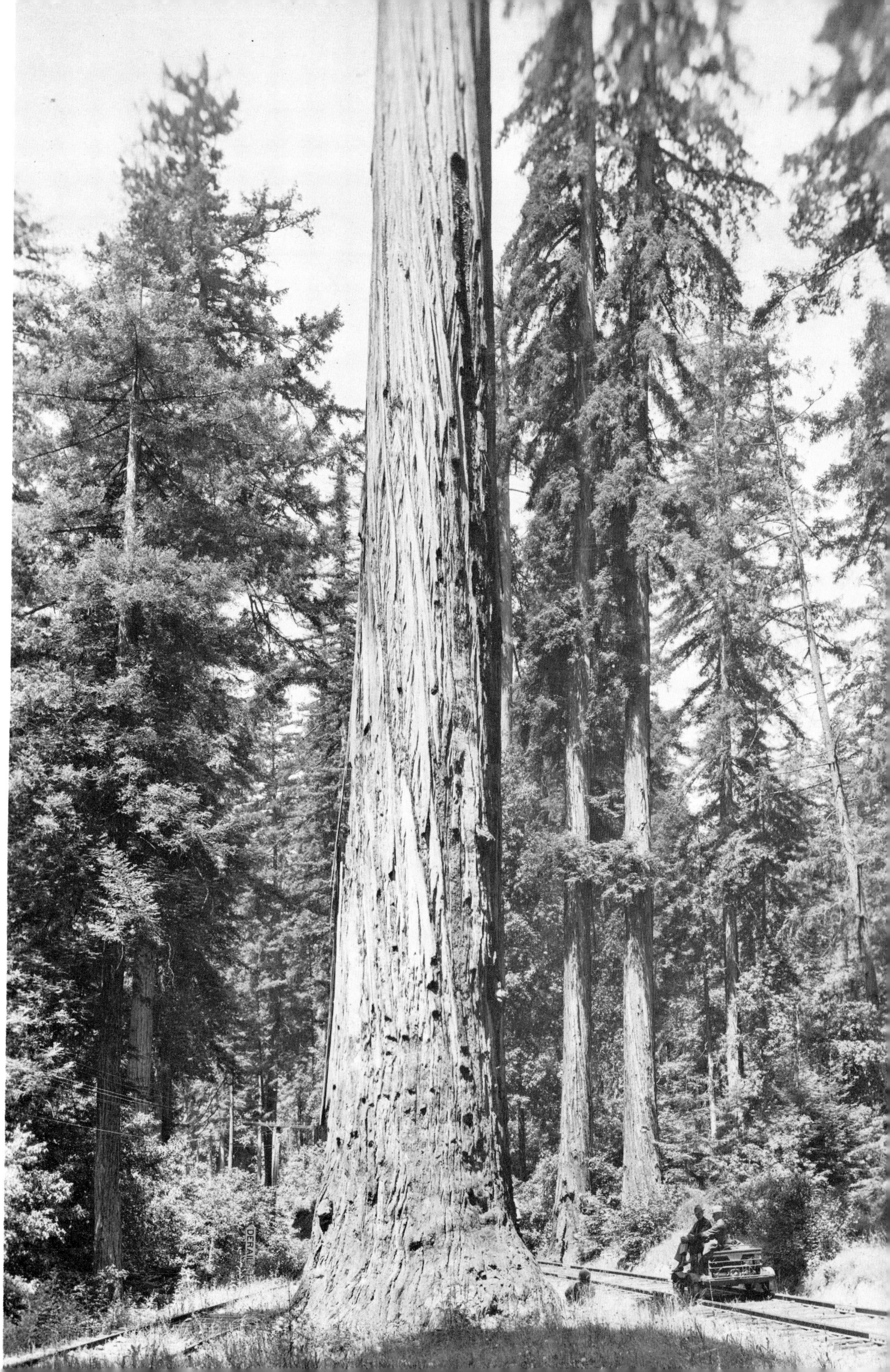

CALIFORNIA WESTERN RAILROAD COLLECTION

	NORTH SHORE R. R.	
* Daily	SAN FRANCISCO AND CAZADERO.	g No stop on Sun.
a Monday only		§ Saturday only
‡ Sunday and Legal Holidays		c Daily except Monday
† Daily except Saturday and Sunday		d Daily except Sunday and Monday

PM	PM	PM	AM	AM	Mls	Lv June 12, 1910 Ar	AM	AM	PM	PM
‡7 15	†5 45	§2 45	*8 15	‡9 15	0	..SAN FRANCISCO..	8 05	11 05	8 05	7 35
7 55	6 25	3 25	8 55	9 55	6	...SAUSALITO....	7 22	10 22	7 22	6 52
8 20	6 50	3 50	9 20	10 20	16	...SAN ANSELMO...	7 00	10 00	7 00	6 30
8 28	6 56	3 56	9 26	10 26	17	....Fairfax....	6 52	9 52	6 52	g6 22
8 40	7 09	4 09	9 40	10 40	21	....Whiteshill....	6 40	9 40	6 40	g6 11
8 44	7 13	4 13	9 44	10 44	22	...San Geronimo..	6 37	9 35	6 37	g6 08
8 49	7 18	4 18	9 49	10 49	24	....Lagunitas....	6 32	9 30	6 32	g6 03
8 56	7 25	4 25	9 56	10 56	27	..CAMP TAYLOR..	6 24	9 20	6 21	g5 52
9 06	7 35	4 35	10 06	11 06	30	...Tocaloma....	6 15	9 10	6 09	g5 40
9 20	7 50	4 53	10 24	11 21	35	..POINT REYES...	*6 00	8 55	‡5 55	g5 25
PM	PM	5 08	10 36	AM	40	...Millerton....	AM	8 40	PM	PM
.....	.....	5 21	10 49	.....	44	....Marshall....		8 26	.....	4 52
.....	.....	5 36	11 01	.....	48	....Hamlet.....		8 14		4 37
.....	.....	5 42	11 16	.....	54	...TOMALES.....		8 03		4 26
.....	.....	5 58	11 23	.....	57	....Fallon....		7 47		4 16
.....	.....	6 10	11 36	.....	58	.VALLEY FORD...		7 35		4 01
.....	.....	6 16	11 43	.....	61	BODEGA ROADS...		7 25	==	3 51
===	.....	6 21	11 48	.....	63	...Freestone....		7 20	AM	3 47
AM	.....	6 37	12 03	.....	67	...Occidental....		7 08	9 55	3 35
*10 05	.....	6 42	12 08	.....	68	..Camp Meeker...		7 01	9 50	3 27
10 10	.....	6 57	12 23	.....	72	....Tyrone.....		6 46	9 36	3 11
10 25	.....	7 04	12 29	.....	73	...Monte Rio....	==	6 46	9 31	3 08
10 30	.....	7 08	12 32	.....	74	..Mesa Grande...	PM	6 35	9 27	3 02
10 34	.....	7 30	12 40	.....	76	.DUNCAN MILLS..	5 00	6 26	9 20	2 55
10 58	.....	7 55	1 05	.....	83	...CAZADERO...	*4 35	a6 00	*8 55	*2 30
11 23	.....	AM	PM	.....		Ar	Lv PM	AM	AM	PM

Additional train Lv San Anselmo ‡4 20 PM. Ar Point Reyes 5 25 PM. Lv Point Reyes ‡2 55 PM. Ar San Anselmo 4 00 PM.

SANTA FE SYSTEM
(Los Angeles Division)
LOS ANGELES, SANTA ANA AND SAN DIEGO

PM	AM	PM	PM	AM	Mls	Lv June 14, 1910 Ar	PM	PM	AM	PM	AM
*5 05	*1055	*1201	*2 15	*8.55	0	..LOS ANGELES..	1 00	6 10	6.45	1030	8 20
5 54	11 41	12.50	3 01	9 47	27	....Anaheim....	12.09	.....	5.50	9 38	7 28
6 08	11 55	1.03	3 15	10.03	31	....Orange.....	12.01	5 13	5.40	9 30	7 20
6 15	AM	1.10	3 23	10.10	34	...Santa Anna..	11.45	5 05	5.30	9 20	*715
PM	.....	2.55	5 00	11.45	85	..Oceanside...	10.02	3 30	3.45	7 50	.....
.....	.....	4.30	6 30	1.10	126	..San Diego...	8.35	*200	2.15	6 30	.....
.....	.....	4.55	6 50		132	.National City..	*7.50	.....	1.30	*550	.....
		AM	PM				AM	PM	AM		

Timetable from Bancroft's Railway Guide listed rail connections up the coast from San Francisco. Early day Fort Bragg residents reached the rails by stagecoach that travelled over rugged roads.

gers continued to dream of the day when comfortable railroad cars would roll all the way to San Francisco. Commenting on Northwestern Pacific construction progress (which actually was slowing because of the Depression), the Fort Bragg Advocate reported:[3]

> The Northwestern Pacific gap of 110 miles from Willits northbound to Pepperwood will require a year to build. During that time, however, the 12 mile gap may be closed to connect Willits and Fort Bragg.

What the CWR lacked in speed of construction, it made up in the quality. Redwood lumber, preferred over pine for railway ties because of its durability, came of course from the Union mills. The initial construction was with sixty-five pound rails, relatively heavy for a short-haul line of the day.

The mountainous terrain was the CWR's greatest enemy during construction. Longer railroads ordinarily had extensive flat stretches to cover, a fact that helped absorb higher costs of pushing tracks through rougher terrain.

Since virtually the entire route from Fort Bragg to Willits was mountainous, the tracks necessarily wound up slopes and around curves.

It would take forty miles to reach its destination only 22 airline miles away.

As a result of the terrain the CWR route was

3. Fort Bragg Advocate, April 10, 1907.

Overhead "A" frames supported this California Western bridge and reduced the possibility of damage from logs in the river. Tracks crossed and recrossed the river as they made their way toward Willits.

Locomotive No. 4, carrying passengers after its 1904 acquisition, arrived in Fort Bragg by ship. The railroad's first locomotives were used in helping to build the tracks through the mountains to Willits.

relatively steep; grades ranged up to 3.3 per cent as compared to a maximum of one per cent on most railroads.

There were countless curves as the tracks, hugging the natural route of the Noyo River canyon, stretched deeper into the mountains. The tracks crossed back and forth over the river to take advantage of the most favorable terrain.

Construction engineers twisted the tracks according to the commands of the mountainous terrain. Many thirty-three and thirty-four degree curves — usually sharp for a railroad — carried the tracks through the forest.

One trestle curved in a perfect letter "S" to help conquer the mountain route.

So steep was the way that in one area it was necessary for the tracks to stretch more than eight miles to cover a 1½-mile distance.

But the California Western tracks pushed on toward Willits regardless of mountain obstacles.

Construction of the California Western mounted to an expensive project — probably much more costly than the records showed.

The CWR was capitalized at $1 million (the Union Lumber Company owned all of the stock). This would have valued the railroad and its equipment at $40,000 a mile — substantially less than the $100,000 per mile average capitalization for most railroads. A 1921 report placed the CWR's value at $2 million, and undoubtedly this figure was quite conservative.[4]

Engineers estimated construction of the Northwestern Pacific line would cost $150,000 per mile; there is every reason to believe that the price tag for

4. Financial reports relative to operations of the California Western Railroad are based on information released annually in standard financial references, including "Walker's Manual of California Securities," (H. D. Walker Company, San Francisco) and "Moody's Steam Railroad Manual," (Moody's Investors Service, New York).

47

Equipment is assembled for cementing the interior of Tunnel No. 2, last barrier for the California Western Railroad's route from the Pacific Ocean to Willits.

building the California Western, going through much rougher terrain, was substantially higher.

A 1914 California Railroad Commission report reflected the high construction costs and value of the California Western line. The company estimated that the cost for replacing the entire railroad system would be $1,876,860. The state agency — which often halved inflated valuations placed by other railways on their property — very nearly agreed. The commission estimated that the price tag for reproducing the CWR tracks and equipment would be $1,724,900.

Unquestionably the profits from logging as the rails pushed through the redwood forests helped to make the project worthwhile, as did the hope of achieving transcontinental connections that would assist in marketing the timber.

Regardless of costs, the CWR pushed onward. The tracks reached Burbeck, 27.8 miles from Fort Bragg, in 1910, and the main reason they were not extended immediately to Willits was obvious. The final few miles were the most difficult along the entire route.

Although the distance from Burbeck to Willits was but five miles as the crow flies, there were steep grades for the engineers to conquer. It would take nearly 12 miles of track to wind through the mountains. Even at that it would be an engineering feat.

Despite the mighty grades and huge expenses, Fort Bragg needed the rail outlet for its residents and lumber products. The decision was made in late 1910 to construct the final link to Willits. Engineers agreed that a second tunnel on the line would conquer the mountains.

The contract for what was described as an 840 foot tunnel (it proved to be 795 feet long when completed) was awarded in April, 1911, to Nelson and Company of San Francisco.

By this time the efficient Chinese railroad workers generally had gone into other employment. The Fort Bragg Advocate reported:[5]

> The contractors are experienced men and they intend to employ only white men on the work. It will take five months to finish the tunnel and by that time the railroad will be connected up at both ends. The east portal of the tunnel is about four miles due west of Willits.

Work on the tunnel proceeded rapidly, for both townspeople and lumbering interests were eager for the prestige and usefulness of the railroad. Eighty men were employed and they were divided into four crews for work on two shifts of twelve hours each from both ends of the tunnel.

The tunnel was completed on schedule and the tracks were stretched through it early in November, 1911.

The great day that Fort Bragg had awaited for nearly a quarter of a century was approaching.

---

5. Fort Bragg Advocate, April 26, 1911.

This Studebaker automobile was equipped with rail wheels so it could operate on the Glen Blair Lumber Company railway, which connected with the California Western tracks. Pictured here are members of the Blair family touring their redwood empire on a spring day in 1913.

*Stretching through the magnificent redwood forests,
the tracks of the California Western reached Willits
late in 1911 and beckoned travelers to enjoy the trip.*

This historic picture was taken December 19, 1911, as Locomotive No. 5 rolled from Fort Bragg to Willits with the first passengers to travel the new redwood route awaited many years by residents.

6. Iron Horse Meets Iron Horse

The California Western's tracks reached Willits as 1911 was drawing to a close. While the new roadbed had not yet been ballasted, CWR officials decided that it was time to treat Fort Bragg residents to their first ride over the long awaited steel highway.

Willits, a city of 1,200 people, already was on the Northwestern Pacific main line stretching from San Francisco. Tracks were being pushed toward Eureka.

December 19, was set as the date for the premiere trek on the completed route. Fort Bragg was receiving its greatest Christmas present six days ahead of time.

The railroad's extension had been the prime subject of talk for months in the city's business circles, lodges, women's club meetings, and in the logging camps. Everyone in Fort Bragg wanted to be among the first to ride behind the Iron Horse on its historic initial trip through the redwoods and over the mountains to Willits.

But even by installing benches on three flat cars to supplement the seats in the two passenger coaches, there would be room for only 150 fortunate passengers.

The task of selecting the chosen few from the city's 2,500 residents went to F. C. White, Union's

51

superintendent at the time and later president of the California Western. Those lucky enough to be invited for the trip rode free as guests of the California Western and the Union Lumber Company.

The few receiving invitations regarded the honor as something akin to knighthood. Undoubtedly, considerable status in Fort Bragg went to the person who could boast he or she had been beckoned to make the historic trip.

Directing the premiere train's actual operation was J. C. French, CWR superintendent.

Early in the morning of December 19, the crowds began arriving at the Fort Bragg depot. The people fortunate enough to have been invited for the trip climbed aboard the cars. Those not so lucky inspected the train and dreamed when they, too, could ride

John Pimentel (left) and Fred Hanson, pictured in later years, were brakeman and conductor respectively on first passenger train from Fort Bragg to Willits.

The crowd at Willits which gave an enthusiastic welcome to the first train from Fort Bragg in 1911 posed for this historic picture shortly after the travelers arrived.

CALIFORNIA WESTERN RAILROAD COLLECTION

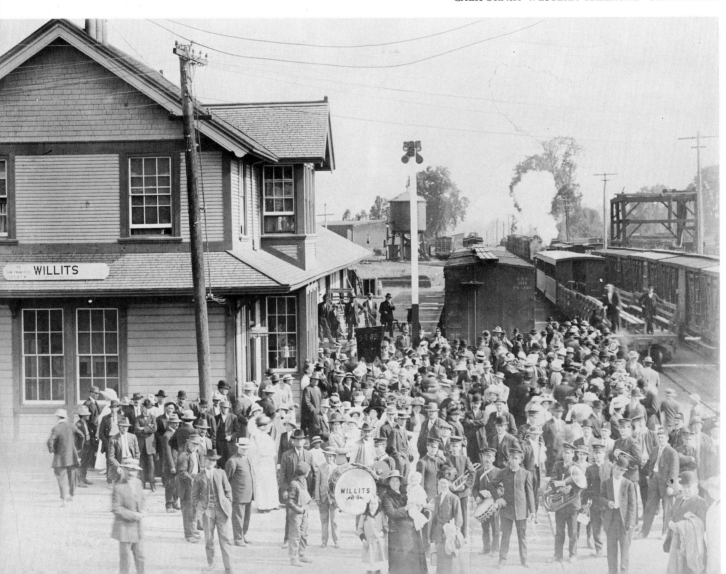

Passengers enjoy one of the many excursion trips between Fort Bragg and Willits which attracted San Francisco area residents when the line was completed.

over the mountains to Willits as well as miles of track stretching from there across the nation.

Ed Hendrickson was the locomotive engineer for the trip. Assisting operations were brakeman John Pimentel, who left his birthplace in the Azores when a youth to settle in the United States. He found the redwoods and fell in love with them. So anxious was he to settle in Fort Bragg that he eagerly took a job laying tracks for the California Western. His eagerness was rewarded in just nine days with a position as a CWR trainman.

The conductor was Fred Hanson, who had joined the California Western in 1905 after work on other logging railroads. Hanson in later years recalled the occasion happily as "quite a day."[1]

---

1. John Pimentel and Fred Hanson proudly watched the California Western achieve fame as a railroad and in 1963 — still residents of Fort Bragg — they recalled the first trip to Willits and other details of the CWR's history during interviews with the author.

The appointed 9:15 a.m. departure time arrived, and Mr. Hanson called the traditional "all aboard" — even though the eager riders long had been aboard.

The engine's bell rang happily; its horn gave a deep blast. The passengers cheered, and so did the bystanders left behind to make the trip another day.

The train chugged from the depot, its ringing bell almost drowned out by cheers.

While Hendrickson sat in the cab as official engineer, French took the throttle for the happy and historic trip.

The honor of pulling the first travelers over the completed route went to Engine No. 5, a 90,000 pound Schenectady Locomotive Company product built in 1880 and acquired in 1906 by the CWR.

The train rolled along the familiar and ever beautiful route by Pudding Creek, through Tunnel No. 1, and then alongside the Noyo River. It passed Alpine, Irmulco, and Burbeck. Then it began to move through territory that was unfamiliar to the passengers. Ahead was the recently completed Tunnel No. 2.

The passengers cheered.

Once through the tunnel, the train began to descend towards Willits.

Reflecting the feelings of its readers, The Fort Bragg Advocate reported the occasion of the first trip to Willits with the headline, "A Great Day of Rejoicing."

"It was a day looked forward to for years by the old residents of Fort Bragg with eager anticipation," The Advocate's editor wrote, "and when it did finally come, it brought with it all the pleasure and happiness of years stored up in realization of such an important event.

"It was a great day in the broadest sense of the word," continued the editor, warming up to the subject, "and those in that party — we venture — will always refer to it as one of the most happy moments of their lives, when the coast of Mendocino County was bound with steel rails, on one of the grandest and most scenic routes in the State of California, with the interior, giving direct communication with the outside world."

The Advocate's editor described the trip with detail and enthusiasm.

"There is loop after loop on the road before reaching the summit," he reported. "The construction presented some very difficult engineering problems . . . This part of the road is simply grand from a scenic point of view, and will be the tourists' delight after the road is opened up next spring for travel . . ."

The editor wrote no truer words as he described the scenery, for the line was to delight travelers for many decades to come.

The locomotive's whistle echoed over the countryside, alerting nearly everyone. An eager crowd was waiting at Willits, and the town's community band began to play as the Iron Horse from the shores of the Pacific chugged into town.

The passengers were so thrilled they hardly noticed that the lack of ballast on new sections of the track made the last part of the trip a bit rough.

Pages in the 1913 Bancroft's Railway Guide offered helpful advice to travelers and also advertised the hotels and shops awaiting visitors in San Francisco.

54

CALIFORNIA WESTERN RAILROAD COLLECTION

Departure of Locomotive No. 5 proudly pulling passenger coaches 42 and 43 became a familiar sight in Fort Bragg after the completed route to Willits was opened.

By the time the train reached Willits, tooting whistles and ringing bells on Northwestern Pacific locomotives were joining the band's musical welcome.

"Old men acted in playful moods like boys," reported The Advocate, "and the whole population was enthusiastic in the demonstration made."

The Iron Horse from the Pacific had arrived.

Highlighting the celebration was a lunch at the Hotel Willits attended by C. R. Johnson and his daughter, Emily.

For the return to Fort Bragg, Mr. French again took the throttle of the locomotive, handling it, The Advocate reported, "very carefully over the road, proving himself to be a master mechanic in his line."

That evening the railroad played host for a banquet at Fort Bragg's Hotel Windsor. Still rollicking, townspeople then celebrated the great occasion with a dance in Red Men's Hall.

One person missing from the Fort Bragg celebration, however, was the CWR's superintendent,

J. C. French. While outwardly calm during the trek, he had been concerned over his passengers' safety on sections of the unballasted track. He excused himself from the festivities in order to recover from a headache.

There were few automobiles at the time, particularly in the rugged mountains along the Mendocino Coast where roads were few and poor. The completion of the railroad heralded a new era of easier travel for passengers and more accessible markets for the region's timber.

Despite the success of the initial trip and The Advocate editor's prediction that service would start in the spring, Fort Bragg had to wait for more fun on its new steel highway. The winter proved to be a wet one. Heavy rains not only delayed the ballasting but also brought landslides.

The railroad was regarded as safe enough for regular traffic only by mid-summer of 1912, a full six months after its unofficial opening.

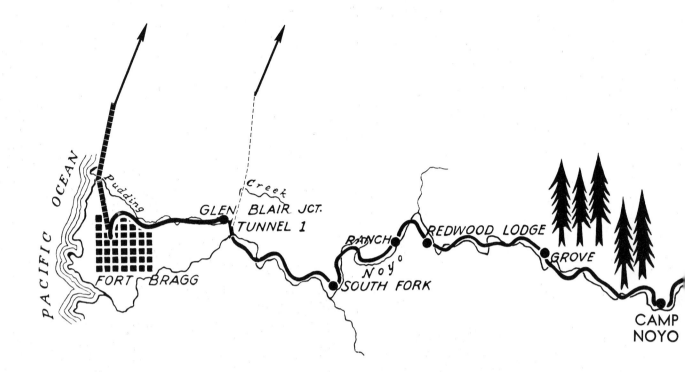

DISTANCE	STATIONS	ELEVATIONS
.0	Fort Bragg	80
1.0	Pudding Creek	20
3.4	Glen Blair Jct.	27
6.6	South Fork	39
9.0	Ranch	64
10.0	Redwood Lodge	78
12.7	Grove	125
15.0	Camp Three	199
16.0	Camp Four	228
16.4	Camp Noyo	229
18.1	Alpine	264
20.0	Camp Seven	292
20.5	Noyo Lodge	308
21.3	Northspur	322
23.9	Irmulco	408
26.8	Shake City	560
27.7	Burbeck	688
28.7	Soda Springs	808
30.4	Clare Mill	1,023
32.6	Crowley	1,375
33.8	Crater	1,513
35.4	Summit	1,740
37.5	Rodgers	1,433
40.0	Willits	1,364

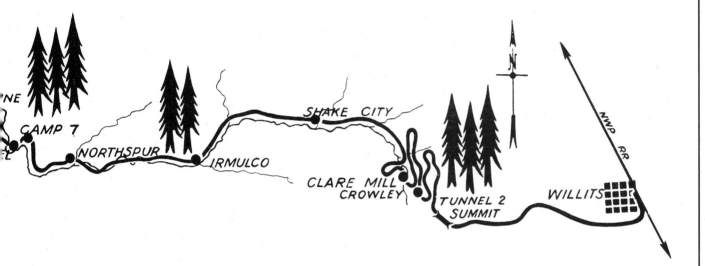

'NE

CAMP 7

NORTHSPUR

IRMULCO

SHAKE CITY

CLARE MILL
CROWLEY

TUNNEL 2
SUMMIT

N

NWP RR

WILLITS

*This map shows the completed route of the California
Western Railroad stretching forty miles from Fort
Bragg to Willits, where it connected with the Northwestern Pacific Railroad. The chart at left lists stations, distances, and elevations on the winding railroad through the redwood forests and mountains.*

These happy travelers boarded flat cars converted for passenger use to join one of many CWR excursions scheduled when the railroad was completed.

The first through trip open to the general public was headed for a Fourth of July celebration at Willits.

"This is a great chance to take a ride over the new road," reported The Fort Bragg Advocate, "running through great redwoods and spend a day with our neighbors."

The Iron Horse left Fort Bragg at 7 a.m, arriving in Willits at 9:30 a.m. for a day marked with basket lunches, fireworks, sport events, and the inevitable patriotic speeches. The return trip departed from Willits at 6 a.m.

A special inducement to acquaint the public with the line provided round-trip tickets for $3 — the usual cost for traveling just one way. The CWR announced that those wishing to stay more than a day and return by rails would be charged $4.50, a bargain rate when compared to the fees for riding the less thrilling stagecoaches.

A week later, on July 10, a reverse version of the first excursion came. A special train ran from Willits to introduce residents to the charms of seaside Fort Bragg.

The completed railroad line helped people of the two cities get acquainted. It also brought new commerce to Fort Bragg. The Advocate proudly noted on July 17 that the first passenger train carrying a freight car rolled over the route. The cargo was eighty-two barrels of wine bound from Cloverdale to Fort Bragg.

The CWR tracks at Willits met those of the Northwestern Pacific, already stretching from San Francisco and being pushed northward to Eureka. As a result, the California Western attracted more than exclusively residents of various Mendocino

County communities. The people of San Francisco were enchanted with the redwood country. The CWR provided convenient means into the redwoods, for special trains carried passengers from the bay area.

By late July, the CWR attracted a crowd of four hundred San Franciscans in a single day.

"The many excursionists were given full benefit of California's grandest scenery on the California Western Railroad and Navigation Company's open air observation cars," The Advocate reported, referring no doubt to the flat cars topped with improvised chairs, "and every moment of the ride through the virgin redwoods of the upper Noyo and along its winding way."

Even the residents of the redwood country never tired of its charms.

"Each and every member of the party was loud in its praises of the scenic beauty of the new road," the newspaper noted proudly.

Rail travelers gave a most enthusiastic reception to the new route. Passenger ticket sales brought the California Western $37,422 in the fiscal year ending June 30, 1912 — the year before opening of the line to Willits. The following year passenger revenue nearly doubled, with the CWR collecting $60,126 for fares on the scenic trip through the redwoods.

Word of the beautiful, winding railroad trip spread rapidly. In 1916, despite the growing popularity of automobiles, passengers paid $63,765 to ride the California Western. While many riders were Fort Bragg residents, thousands of the passengers were visitors coming to see the beauty of the redwoods.

Virtually every railway in America drew new settlers to its area, for the presence of the steel highways greatly increased the desirability of any region. The CWR's completion was no exception to the rule. The line was seized upon as an ideal reason for settlers and investors to acquire property destined for development with the expected population boom.

The Union Lumber Company offered numerous parcels of cleared land for sale to be developed into

Fort Bragg's name rated only small print in top map from Sunset Magazine in 1910, prior to completion of the route to Willits. The city's name achieved prominence in bottom map, appearing three years later when rails linked Fort Bragg to the continent.

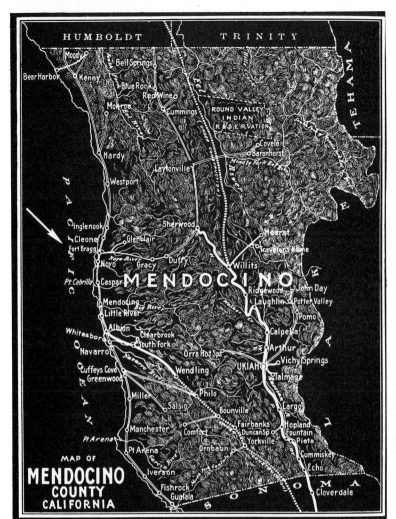

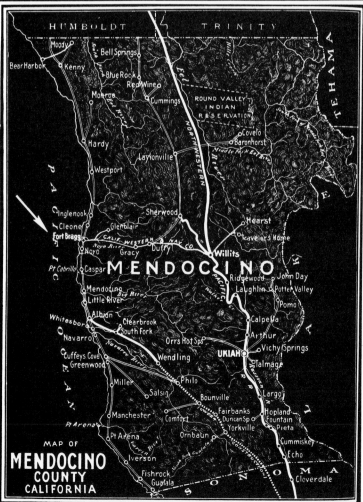

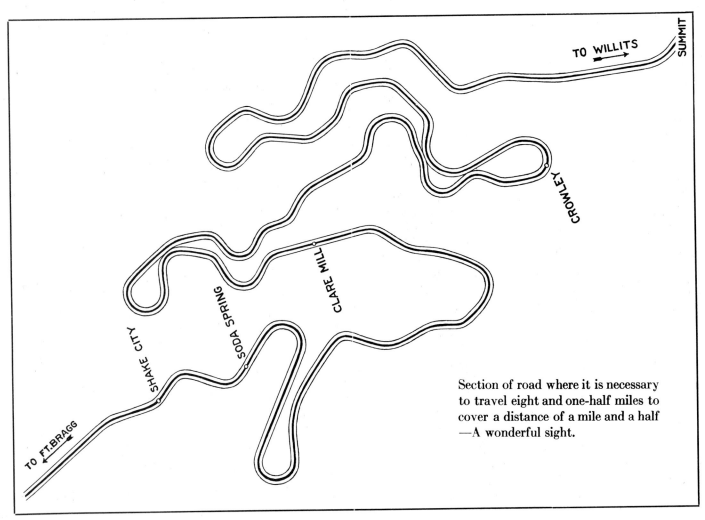

Section of road where it is necessary to travel eight and one-half miles to cover a distance of a mile and a half —A wonderful sight.

STATIONS, DISTANCES, ELEVATION, Etc.

DISTANCE	STATIONS	ELEVATION
.0	Fort Bragg	80
f 1.0	Pudding Creek	20
f 3.4	Glen Blair Jct.	27
f 6.7	South Fork	39
f 9.0	Ranch	64
f 10.0	Redwood Lodge	78
f 12.6	Grove	125
f 15.0	Camp Three	199
f 16.0	Camp Four	228
f 18.0	Alpine	264
f 20.0	Camp Seven	292
f 20.5	Noyo Lodge	308
21.2	Northspur	322
f 21.3	Noyo River Tavern	330
23.9	Irmulco	408
f 26.7	Shake City	560
f 27.7	Burbeck	688
f 28.7	Soda Springs	808
f 30.2	Clare Mill	1023
f 32.6	Crowley	1375
f 33.8	Crater	1513
f 35.2	Summit	1740
f 37.5	Rodgers	1433
40.0	Willits	1364

DISTANCE	STATIONS		ELEVATION
.0	Willits	N.W.P.	1364
25.55	Ukiah	"	610
54.31	Cloverdale	"	315
71.51	Healdsburg	"	99
85.76	Santa Rosa	"	151
137.87	San Francisco	"	4

DISTANCE	STATIONS	ELEVATION
.0	Fort Bragg	80
1.0	Pudding Creek	20
3.4	Glen Blair Jct.	27
6.5	Glen Blair	130

f—Train stops only on signal or to leave passengers.
Passenger train service in either direction daily.
Connects with the Northwestern Pacific Railroad at Willits.
Stage connections are made at Fort Bragg for points up and down the coast.

California Western Railroad and Navigation Company

FORT BRAGG, CALIFORNIA

1011 Crocker Bldg., San Francisco, Cal., Phone Sutter 6170

Issued 1917

residential, dairying, or orchard property. Real estate brokers eagerly took up the sales pitch.

Typical was a newspaper advertisement placed by a San Francisco real estate man named J. L. Johnson:[2]

> Fort Bragg is growing fast and has all the facilities that can be found in any modern town . . . 18 miles from Willits, the California Western Railroad and Navigation Company have sub-divided 2,000 acres of cut overland with the idea of attracting the best class of settlers, and every facility will be offered by the railway company to see that any one who purchases this land is aided in getting properly, comfortably, and profitably settled.

The railroad's completion came at a time when California's romanticized charm was hitting a peak. Thousands of midwesterners and easterners were making the trek to the Golden State to establish new homes. Many were wealthy people attracted by the climate and scenery; others hoped to amass riches as they basked in the sun. While there were no mass arrivals of migrants to Fort Bragg (cooler than southern portions of the state despite its scenic grandeur), numerous settlers were attracted who would have gone elsewhere had it not been for the California Western.

When autumn came, it was quite logical that Fort Bragg Day at the Mendocino County Fair in Willits would attract record crowds.

And it was most logical that the Iron Horse from the Pacific would carry the crowds — at a bargain rate of just $3 for the round trip — in comfortable coaches through the unsurpassed redwoods.

---

2. Fort Bragg Advocate, August 28, 1912.

The wonders of the rail route through the redwoods were depicted in a 1917 folder issued by the California Western. Section at left gave prospective travelers an idea of the twisting route and listed mileages as well as elevations relative to the Fort Bragg trip and the route to San Francisco. Illustration at right showed an excursion train stopping so that passengers could look down on tracks where they would travel on the winding way through the mountains.

Where one track is almost directly over the track lower down.

16

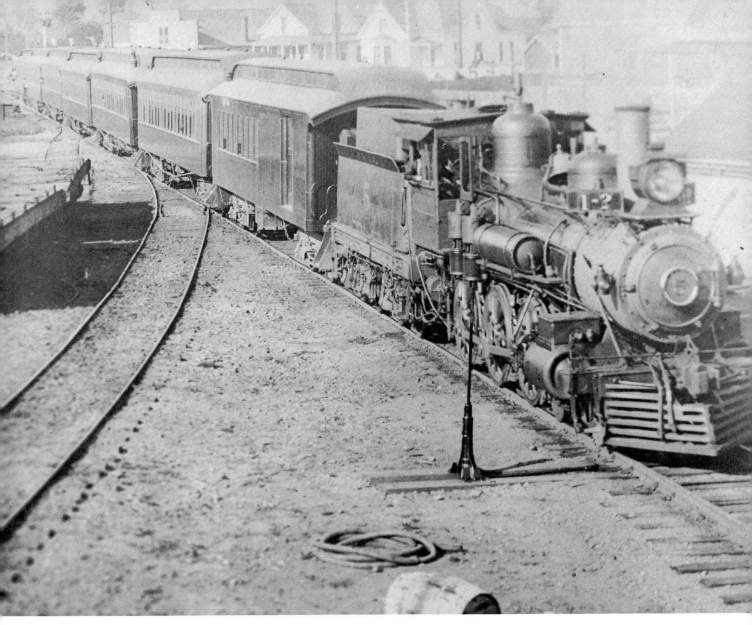

Locomotive No. 5 pulls a train of five passenger coaches with visitors from the San Francisco area to Fort Bragg. Trains used short coaches in order to negotiate the many sharp curves on the winding route.

Snow, which occasionally falls on the higher elevations of the CWR route, prompted a train to stop by a water tower for a picture during a trip in about 1917.

7. *Metropolis in the Redwoods*

Hardly more than a quarter of a century saw Fort Bragg rise from an abandoned military post into a city noted for its redwood mills as well as a business district serving a sizable trading area. While the redwoods were the basic economic factor, unquestionably the convenience of the California Western was a big contributor to the growth.

After the railroad was completed, its right- of-way also served to carry telephone wires to Fort Bragg as still another link in communications.

New residents arrived daily on the CWR, relegating stagecoaches to the museum. It was pleasant to ride the train. Leaving at 8:30 a.m., one arrived just two hours and twenty minutes later at Willits. Here was the connection with the Northwestern Pacific train to Sausalito, just a ferry's ride from San Francisco.

CWR service was so regular that one Fort Bragg haberdasher, A. L. Wintzen, advertised "tailored clothes built on railroad time" to assure customers there would be no waiting.

Among the few interruptions for service to Willits were those coming early in 1914 when a series of storms swept over the Mendocino Coast. An observer reported nine inches of rain fell at one point in thirty-six hours. The swollen Noyo River wiped out two bridges, took out a 180-foot trestle,

ILLUSTRATED

CALIFORNIA WESTERN RAILROAD & NAVIGATION C⁰

THRO THE REDWOODS

CAMPING HUNTING FISHING

and caused a 150-foot landslide near Clare Mill, thirty miles from Fort Bragg.[1]

CWR superintendent C. A. Curtis rallied all available men and H. A. Brown, in charge of rebuilding the bridges, announced trains would be running again within ten days.

The elements battled the workers, however, and the first storm was followed in a few days by another downpour. Logs somersaulted down the Noyo, taking out another bridge. Undaunted, the repair crews worked on and CWR officials predicted they would have trains rolling within two weeks.[2]

"The company is to be complimented upon the earnest manner (with) which the work is being rushed," commented The Fort Bragg Advocate.

True to their word, the CWR officials had the line operating on February 4.

Fort Bragg's pride was its railroad, and the luxury and convenience of California Western passenger service was unquestioned. But there was something lacking while visitors awaited the Northwestern Pacific at Willits.

This particular need was a station befitting the glory of the surrounding redwoods.

When the NWP link from Willits to Eureka was completed in 1915, more passengers passed the area on the run from San Francisco to Seattle.

Even before these visitors began arriving, Mendocino County residents expressed concern that the arrivals would not be sufficiently impressed by their stopover because the Willits depot was plain and unimaginative — typical of those on most railroads.

After conferring with NWP officials, civic leaders obtained an agreement for a remedy. Its preparations began in 1913, just a year after the California Western started serving Willits.

For three years the Union Lumber Company and two other area logging firms set aside clear grain redwood — the most desirable milled, for it had no imperfections or knots. It was reserved for a new depot at Willits.

In 1916 the station was opened and its beauty served as a tribute to the redwood kingdom it served.

Built along picturesque Tyrolean lines of architecture, the depot looked more like a mountain lodge than a conventional station. NWP passengers pro-

---

1. Fort Bragg Advocate, January 7, 1914.

2. Fort Bragg Advocate, January 23, 1914.

The cover of this 1917 CWR brochure suggested the attractions awaiting rail travelers to the redwoods.

Constructed of choice redwood, the depot at Willits served the CWR and the Northwestern Pacific. The structure, built along Tyrolean lines, was regarded as one of America's most beautiful railway stations.

claimed it the most beautiful depot in America. The station served a dual purpose: in addition to waiting facilities, it contained a dining room to feed the hungry passengers riding the California Western and Northwestern Pacific, neither of which boasted dining cars.

The CWR, its steel highway connecting to the transcontinental lines, enabled Fort Bragg residents to boast that they were residents of a metropolis in the redwood kingdom. Larger print was used to designate Fort Bragg's name on nationally circulated maps following completion of the rail links. Townspeople discovered new horizons, for they could proudly purchase a ticket in Fort Bragg for a rail trip across the nation.

The Iron Horse from the Pacific opened immense vistas and made Fort Bragg's dream come true.

The years following completion of the route to Willits brought increased growth for the California

Western as well as its parent, the Union Lumber Company.

Redwood gained in popularity as a building material throughout the nation. The market for redwood expanded particularly through trends for large houses boasting sides shingled with redwood.

Railroads throughout the nation used the more durable redwood ties to replace those of pine as they repaired and rebuilt rights-of-way.

The need for more redwood prompted the CWR to build its Ten Mile River branch in 1916 and 1917. The route was from Fort Bragg northward along the coast to Ten Mile River; it then followed the river inland to redwood forests.

Passenger service on the Ten Mile River branch was limited to loggers enroute to work.

Efficient passenger service on the main line to Willits was giving the CWR an important place in the community's social as well as economic life.

A train rolls alongside the Pacific Ocean enroute to Fort Bragg on the CWR's Ten Mile River Branch, which served a Union Lumber logging area.

Most logging railroads of the era contented themselves in daily duties of hauling timber.

The California Western performed logging chores, but it did much more.

The CWR brought commercial travelers to Fort Bragg and carried the city's residents to the outside world. Sightseers from the San Francisco area found the railroad a most convenient means of enjoying the redwoods — perennially an attraction even for California's natives.

As the years passed, more and more out-of-state visitors learned the glory of the redwoods. Travelwise passengers on the Northwestern Pacific made stopovers in Willits so they could ride the famed CWR route through the forests amid the spectacular mountains.

Appropriately, California Western's official slogan became "The Redwood Route." The slogan helped distinguish the red and black circular insignia emblazoned on the CWR's freight cars and stationery.

Status as a common carrier also earned the California Western the right of exchanging passes with other railroads, ranging from short lines such as itself to transcontinental railways.

The era's pass privilege custom enabled employees of short lines throughout America to travel on railroads without charge across the nation. In exchange, those associated with the transcontinental lines found themselves with passes valid for the dubious right to ride short lines — many of them mining or logging railroads in isolated areas where few desired to travel. In some cases, the small roads

A passenger train rounds a curved trestle that became renowned with California Western passengers. The spectacular structure eventually was replaced with a dirt fill when the route was improved.

Travelers wait at a station in the redwoods as a locomotive approaches to take them to Fort Bragg.

California Western Railroad and Navigation Company
1913

Pass James T. Shaw, Asst. Rate Expert

Account R.R.Com. of the State of Calif.

UNTIL DECEMBER 31, 1913
UNLESS OTHERWISE ORDERED AND SUBJECT TO CONDITIONS ON BACK

OVER ALL LINES

No. A 19

GOOD ON PASSENGER TRAINS ONLY

Pacific Electric Railway Co.

NOT GOOD ON MOTOR COACHES | 1940 | No. 18005

Pass

Account — W. S. Taylor — General Traffic Agent, California Western RR & Nav. Co.

OVER ENTIRE SYSTEM

UNTIL DECEMBER 31st, 1940 | UNLESS OTHERWISE ORDERED AND SUBJECT TO CONDITIONS ON BACK

VALID WHEN COUNTERSIGNED BY D. BATMAN OR M. B. MORRIS

PRESIDENT

NORTHWESTERN PACIFIC
RAILROAD COMPANY
1940-1941 — X 870

REDWOOD EMPIRE ROUTE

PASS ---Mr. H. H. Sanborn---

ACCOUNT President, C.W.RR.& N. Co.

BETWEEN ALL STATIONS UNTIL DECEMBER 31, 1941, UNLESS OTHERWISE LIMITED BELOW AND SUBJECT TO CONDITIONS ON BACK.

VALID WHEN COUNTERSIGNED BY T. F. EAGEN
COUNTERSIGNED

PRESIDENT & GENERAL MANAGER

Southern Pacific Lines
IN
1940-1941 TEXAS AND LOUISIANA — GOX 3938

Pass Mr. H. H. Sanborn. - - - President. California Western R.R. & Nav. Co.

EXPIRES DECEMBER 31st, 1941, UNLESS OTHERWISE LIMITED

EXECUTIVE VICE PRESIDENT

THE DENVER AND RIO GRANDE WESTERN RAILROAD COMPANY
WILSON McCARTHY AND HENRY SWAN, TRUSTEES
1941-42 — B 2660

PASS H. H. Sanborn, President California Western RR. & Nav. Co.

UNTIL DECEMBER 31, 1942, UNLESS OTHERWISE ORDERED OR SPECIFIED HEREON AND SUBJECT TO CONDITIONS ON BACK

VALID WHEN COUNTERSIGNED BY J. M. HADDEN OR E. E. EMERSON
COUNTERSIGNED

THIS PASS ACCEPTED BY ME FOR USE SUBJECT TO CONDITIONS ON BACK

TRUSTEE

CALIFORNIA WESTERN RAILROAD AND NAVIGATION CO.
1941-1942 — NO. 3

CALIFORNIA THE REDWOOD ROUTE WESTERN

PASS Mr. H. H. Sanborn, President, Calif. West. R. R. & N. Co.

UNTIL DECEMBER 31, 1942
UNLESS OTHERWISE ORDERED
SUBJECT TO CONDITIONS ON BACK

GENERAL MANAGER

UNION PACIFIC RAILROAD
NOT GOOD ON "STREAMLINERS" OR "FORTY-NINER"
1941 — AX 2113

PASS Mrs. H. H. Sanborn**** Wife of President California Western R.R.& Nav. Co.

OVER ALL LINES UNTIL JANUARY 31, 1942 UNLESS OTHERWISE ORDERED OR SPECIFIED HEREON

ADDRESS San Francisco REQUEST OF hhs d-31

VALID WHEN COUNTERSIGNED BY F. J. ROACH OR B. L. HERBERT

COUNTERSIGNATURE

PRESIDENT

YOSEMITE VALLEY
1937-1938 RAILWAY COMPANY — 302

PASS Mr. W. S. Taylor General Traffic Agent California Western RR & Navigation Co

ADDRESS Fort Bragg

UNTIL DECEMBER 31, 1938
UNLESS OTHERWISE ORDERED
SUBJECT TO CONDITIONS ON BACK

VICE-PRESIDENT AND GENERAL MANAGER

ran no formal passenger service and many had as little as ten miles of track.[1]

Many transcontinental rail officials complained that exchanging passes was decidedly to their disadvantage because of the difference in company trackage and scope of operation.

There probably were few complaints from the transcontinental railroaders who rode the California Western, for even though its line was only forty miles long it passed through a portion of the world's most beautiful and spectacular scenery.

Many railroaders followed the example of travelers who made the trek to enjoy the ride on the CWR "Redwood Route," growing in fame with the years.

Incidentally, California Western employees received somewhat lower pay, at least during the line's early days, than their counterparts on other railroads.

California Railroad Commission reports showed that CWR wages, not including officers' salaries, averaged $2.41 daily in 1912. Men on the McCloud River Railroad, a logging line, averaged a whopping $3 a day, while the Yosemite Valley Railroad — also a short line, paid $2.56 daily. The Northwestern Pacific and Santa Fe railroads paid daily averages of $2.77 and $2.65.

Typical CWR daily wages in 1912 reported by the state agency were $3.26 for engineers, $2.70 for firemen, $3.39 for conductors, and $1.60 for laborers. Comparable salaries for engineers were $5.07 on the Northwestern Pacific and $6.23 on the Santa Fe.

Upward adjustments were made by 1914, either through complaints of the railroaders or generosity of the CWR management with completion of the line to Willits. The California Western's average daily wage climbed to $2.48 and pay scales reported to the railroad commission included $3.56 for engi-

___

1. Regulations regarding pass "exchanges" were tightened in the 1940's, reducing the bonanza whereby railroad employees could travel across the nation virtually without paying fares.

These are typical railroad passes issued by the California Western and in turn received from other railways by CWR employees. Visiting railroaders marvelled at the engineering and beauty of the route.

neers and $2.73 for firemen. Laborers did not fare so well, for the report showed their daily pay as $1.24, a decline of 36 cents in two years.

Regardless of wages, there was no doubt that the California Western was a pleasant railroad upon which to work. The beauty of the redwoods was hailed by trainmen and travelers alike.

While travelers cherished the line, it was most important in carrying the Union Lumber Company's products to market.

Despite its usefulness, the California Western was far from a financial bonanza for its owners even though assuring shipping facilities for the redwood products. Profits were reported, but they varied sharply from year to year and never amounted to a reasonable return on the invested capital.

Profits in 1915 came to $27,071 on operating revenues of $233,818, and the following year when receipts totaled $258,411 the net zoomed to $70,284. But in 1917 — a year when most railroads were profitable — earnings declined to $46,569 — despite revenues of $281,272. Profits in 1918 totaled $65,782, while $44,340 in earnings was reported in 1919.[2]

The rough terrain over which the CWR operated necessarily trimmed profits. Rainfall averaging nearly fifty inches a year in the redwood empire, with much of the downpour coming in torrents during storms, brought landslides and bridge washouts. Maintenance costs soared above railroads fortunate enough to operate in dry areas or flat terrain.

The CWR spent $145,454 on maintenance and other operating costs in 1915, while in 1916 more favorable weather held such expenditures to $111,937. Operational costs soared to $158,210 in 1917, while $162,367 went to operate and maintain the system the following year.

The table of expenditures for operations followed very much a chart showing the rainfall for the area. Storms brought growth for the redwoods, but they usually resulted in costly repairs to the railroad.

Nevertheless, Fort Bragg had its railroad — a steel highway from the Pacific to the rest of America — and usually operated without interruption despite rain and high waters.

___

2. All financial records cited in this book are based on reports filed with the California Railroad Commission (later named the California Public Utilities Commission) and reported annually in Steam Railroad Manual.

MAP
OF THE LINES OF THE
NORTHWESTERN PACIFIC
RAILROAD COMPANY

RMH

SCALE IN MILES

EUREKA
AND VICINITY
SCALE IN MILES

SAUSALITO
AND ADJACENT TERRITORY
SCALE IN MILES

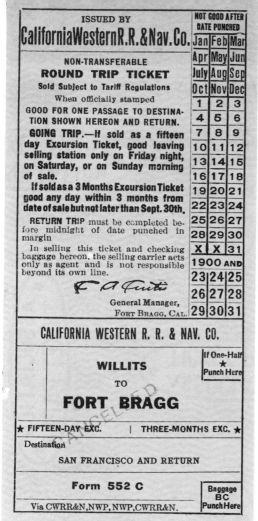

ISSUED BY
California Western R.R. & Nav. Co.

NOT GOOD AFTER DATE PUNCHED

Jan	Feb	Mar
Apr	May	Jun
July	Aug	Sep
Oct	Nov	Dec
1	2	3
4	5	6
7	8	9
10	11	12
13	14	15
16	17	18
19	20	21
22	23	24
25	26	27
28	29	30
X	X	31
1900 AND		
23	24	25
26	27	28
29	30	31

NON-TRANSFERABLE
ROUND TRIP TICKET
Sold Subject to Tariff Regulations
When officially stamped
GOOD FOR ONE PASSAGE TO DESTINA-
TION SHOWN HEREON AND RETURN.

GOING TRIP.—If sold as a fifteen
day Excursion Ticket, good leaving
selling station only on Friday night,
on Saturday, or on Sunday morning
of sale.

If sold as a 3 Months Excursion Ticket
good any day within 3 months from
date of sale but not later than Sept. 30th.

RETURN TRIP must be completed before midnight of date punched in
margin

In selling this ticket and checking
baggage hereon, the selling carrier acts
only as agent and is not responsible
beyond its own line.

F. A. Curtis
General Manager,
FORT BRAGG, CAL.

CALIFORNIA WESTERN R. R. & NAV. CO.

WILLITS
TO
FORT BRAGG

If One-Half ★ Punch Here

★ FIFTEEN-DAY EXC. | THREE-MONTHS EXC. ★

Destination
SAN FRANCISCO AND RETURN

Form 552 C

Baggage BC Punch Here

Via CWRR&N, NWP, NWP, CWRR&N.

NORTHWESTERN PACIFIC RAILROAD CO.

Baggage BC Punch Here

SAN FRANCISCO
TO
WILLITS

★ FIFTEEN-DAY EXC. | THREE-MONTHS EXC. ★

Form 552 C | Not Good If Detached

Destination
SAN FRANCISCO AND RETURN

Issued by C. W. R. R. & N. Co.

If One-half ★ Punch Here

Via CWRR&N, NWP, NWP, CWRR&N.

NORTHWESTERN PACIFIC RAILROAD CO.

If One-half ★ Punch Here

WILLITS
TO
SAN FRANCISCO

★ FIFTEEN-DAY EXC. | THREE-MONTHS EXC. ★

Form 552 C | Not Good If Detached

Destination
SAN FRANCISCO AND RETURN

Issued by C. W. R. R. & N. Co.

Baggage BC Punch Here

Via CWRR&N, NWP, NWP, CWRR&N.

CALIFORNIA WESTERN R. R. & NAV. CO.

Baggage BC Punch Here

FORT BRAGG
TO
WILLITS

★ FIFTEEN-DAY EXC. | THREE-MONTHS EXC. ★

Form 552 C | Not Good If Detached

Destination
SAN FRANCISCO AND RETURN

8. *Wake Up in San Francisco*

One notable lack for the California Western, as it rolled into the 1920's was the Pullman service so famous on the railroads traversing the continent and the Pacific Coast.

This minor deficiency soon was to be remedied so that the CWR could take its place with the greatest of railroads.

Travelers ordinarily left Fort Bragg at 10 a.m., arriving in Willits at 12:30 p.m. If bound to San Francisco — and most passengers were — it was necessary to board the southbound Northwestern Pacific train reaching San Francisco late the same evening.

As a result travelers lost approximately a day in journeying to the bay area. Although only a few years removed from the more tedious trip by stagecoach, sojourners yearned for the luxury of sleeper service.

CWR passenger service was growing by leaps and bounds with the years. In 1918 a total of 19,079 travelers happily rode the Redwood Route, contributing more than twenty per cent of the line's revenue. The following year volume reached 32,465 passengers — an increase of 13,386 — whose fares contributed almost twenty-five per cent of the CWR's revenue.[1]

The era saw Wharton Taylor, the CWR's general traffic agent, selling many tickets not only to San Francisco but also for rail travel across the nation after making the first leg of the journey through the redwoods.

---

1. Passenger volume reported by the California Public Utilities Commission (successor to the California Railroad Commission).

Here is a ticket that would take travelers to San Francisco and back to Fort Bragg via the California Western and its connection with the Northwestern Pacific. For a view of how excursion trains wound back and forth on the famed CWR redwood route, turn the page.

PHOTOGRAPH PAGE FOLLOWING:
CALIFORNIA WESTERN COLLECTION

In 1920 the California Western carried 34,585 passengers — an amazing increase of 15,506 in just two years — and their fares accounted for nearly thirty per cent of the lines receipts.

The 1920 population of Fort Bragg was 3,000, making it obvious that the city's residents and visitors depended on the railroad.

Pullman service seemed a logical innovation to meet the community travel demands.

Officials of the Union Lumber Company and the California Western had negotiated relative to sleeper service via the Northwestern Pacific for several months when the good news was announced in May of 1921.

"Hurrah!" cheered The Advocate in announcing overnight service would start May 29, in time for the summer season traditionally bringing the bulk of visitors to and from the redwood kingdom. "Fort Bragg is to have a Pullman night train service to San Francisco, thanks to the enterprise of the California Western Railroad and Navigation Company. This new service will start May 29, and continue daily thereafter."[2]

The schedule called for the Pullman, along with a baggage coach, to leave Fort Bragg at 9 p.m. arriving in Willits at 11:15 p.m. The southbound Northwestern Pacific train picked up the cars at 2 a.m. and passengers reached San Francisco at 9:05 a.m.

Travelers to Fort Bragg also could enjoy the comforts of a Pullman The northbound schedule provided an 8:45 p.m. departure from San Francisco, with arrival in Fort Bragg at 8:05 a.m.

Townspeople acclaimed the "wake-up in San Francisco" service, as it was advertised, although in reality passengers awoke in Sausalito — just across the bay. In those pre-Golden Gate Bridge days passengers rode ferries for the last lap of the journey.

The joy of Fort Bragg's residents, only a decade ago isolated and largely dependent on stagecoaches, was mirrored in the praise heaped on the service by an Advocate reporter:[3]

This is a wonderful convenience and the enterprise is worthy of all possible patronage.

It can be truly said that a night train is beyond the

expectations of the public. Only a few years ago we had no rail connections with the outside world, and many there were who shook their heads with doubt of such a thing ever coming to pass. Yet the road was put through at an estimated cost of two million dollars and now we are to have a night service.

Almost everyone in town proudly gathered at the depot to view the shiny Pullman car as it left for its first trip. For those who missed the occasion, as well as for townspeople wishing to refresh memories of the happy occasion, The Advocate published this glowing description:

The Pullman car is a large steel coach, and is up to the minute in every respect, being of the same type as those on the run between San Francisco and Los Angeles. It has 27 berths. It represents an investment (of) between $60,000 and $70,000.

The newspaper's list of those distinguished by making the first trip included "Dr. Campbell, J. F. Johnson, L. J. Turner, T. A. Douglas, Mrs. Harker, and R. T. Burns."

The Pullman service proved attractive not only for the Fort Bragg residents bound to San Francisco for business or shopping, but also for many vacationists.

The prestige and comfort of Pullman service accounted for many of the 38,822 passengers who rode the California Western in 1923, when the line carried double the number of travelers riding it a scant four years before.

Passengers on the Pullman trip always received a welcome treat when the train stopped briefly at Northspur, approximately half-way between Fort Bragg and Willits. Hot coffee and doughnuts from Union's camp were brought aboard and served free to the smiling passengers.

The inauguration of the night train did not mean finis for CWR day service. Day trains continued to leave Fort Bragg at 10 a.m., making the return trip from Willits start at 2 p.m. This schedule represented a slight change from initial service on the route.

The comfortable Pullman service helped travelers save approximately a day on the trek to or from San Francisco.

Yet despite the convenience and comfort of the sleeper, the night train left many times, as the 1920's grew older, with most of its berths unoccupied.

---

2. Fort Bragg Advocate, May 25, 1921.
3. Fort Bragg Advocate, May 25, 1921.

A Northwestern Pacific passenger train rolls over a bridge as it heads through the redwood country. The line stretched from Eureka to the San Francisco area.

Ford's Model T had found its way into the redwood kingdom, and with more automobiles better roads were demanded. Motor courts sprang up to serve auto travelers.

By the late 1920's automobiles were becoming a general household item. Fewer people were riding the railroads, particularly Pullmans.

The 1923 volume of 38,822 passengers proved to be the record until the advent of the 1960's when the jovial little Skunk rail bus attracted travelers and gave the California Western a well deserved place in American tradition.

In 1924 the CWR carried 32,299 passengers and the following year it served 29,761 travelers.

The 1928 report showed that the Redwood Route carried just 20,097 passengers — only 1,018 more than a decade before. Few travelers made use of the "wake-up in San Francisco" service.

The last Pullman car left Fort Bragg on November 3, 1929. Reduced sleeper service provided a Pullman only from Willits after chair coach from Fort Bragg. There was insufficient patronage even for this limited service, however, and special Pullmans from Willits were removed from the schedules in May, 1930.

The CWR's Pullman era came and went within a decade.

Mack Rail Bus M-80, which became famous as the Skunk, is pictured soon after it went into service.

BILL PENNINGTON COLLECTION

The Mack rail bus was pictured at the Fort Bragg depot embellished with the "redwood route" emblem after entering CWR service. "M-80" proved an inadequate designation for the vehicle and soon riders and railroaders nicknamed it the "Skunk."

9. *They Named it The Skunk*

Automobiles created tough competition not only for Pullmans but for passenger trains generally. The California Western increasingly noted the decline in passenger revenue that railroads throughout America felt during the Roaring Twenties. The prosperous era prompted more and more people to buy cars, and consequently, rely on them instead of trains for travel.

The CWR's passenger volume reached a peak in 1923 when 38,822 travelers rode the redwood line. From then on, there was a steady decline. In 1924,

the railroad carried 32,299 riders; in 1926, only 28,-112 passengers were reported. The automobile had made such inroads on travel habits by 1928 that only 20,097 passengers — barely 1,000 more than reported a decade before — rode the California Western.

It should be noted that the total number of passengers reported annually included members of logging crews bound for work in the forests. They rode on special company "commuter" tickets. While this service was an important function for the railroad, it hardly warranted the cost of operating complete trains from Fort Bragg to Willits. Early morning trains covering only part of the route were scheduled to take loggers to their working areas. Nevertheless, passenger volume reports included these riders.

(See the Appendix for annual reports of the California Western's passenger volume and revenue.)

Major costs stemmed from huge expenses required to operate the system and maintain it during heavy rains and floods. However, a considerable part of the cost was operating daily passenger trains. Unlike the freight trains assembled as needs arose, the passenger trains ran as scheduled regardless of the number of tickets sold.

And the California Western was selling fewer tickets.

Passenger revenue hit a peak of $86,248 in 1921 and declined steadily thereafter. In 1923, when the 38,822 passengers were reported, revenue from riders was $75,276. Passenger revenue in 1925 totalled $54,450 with 29,761 riding. The revenue dropped to $47,616 in 1927 (when 23,025 passengers rode) and to $26,516 in 1929.

Profits also tumbled, and part of the decline no doubt came from the special costs involved in operating passenger service. While a net of $65,782 was reported in 1918, profits fell to $51,052 in 1921 and $24,838 in 1924 despite increases in total revenue.

The problem was not confined to the California Western. The loss of paying passenger revenue plagued other rail lines as automobiles took more

The Mack rail bus begins service in its new home in the redwoods. The hood of the gasoline powered vehicle was similar in design to Mack trucks used extensively during the 1920's. Right, the M-80 rolls over a Noyo River bridge in the shade of redwoods.

CALIFORNIA WESTERN RAILROAD COLLECTION

travelers on trips. Railways sought means to reduce operating costs.

Most discouraging to railroaders was the cost of operating a steam locomotive pulling coaches occupied by only a handful of fare-paying passengers. A few years before, rail coaches frequently were filled.

Many trains on short routes were cut to a single coach for economy, but railroad companies needed more drastic savings to reduce losses.

Among the proposed solutions came one from a motor vehicle manufacturer, Mack Trucks, Inc., a producer of heavy trucks for commercial use.

Mack suggested that passenger costs could be cut by mounting a gasoline engine-powered bus-type vehicle on rail wheels. The savings would be threefold. First, fewer personnel would be needed because the rail bus driver and conductor would replace the engineer, fireman, conductor, and brakeman required as the minimum crew on a conventional train. Secondly, the comparatively quick pick-up power of the gasoline engine would allow faster starts and stops for commuter traffic. Finally, the only maintenance cost would be for the rail bus instead of a locomotive, tender, and one or more passenger coaches.

Mack began producing the rail buses in 1920,

selling the vehicles to such diverse types of railways as the Chicago, Burlington, and Quincy, the Pennsylvania, and the Havana Central of Cuba.[1]

Steam engines furnished almost all rail power at the time. The motorized buses in a degree were the forerunners of the diesel locomotives introduced in the mid-1930's.

Other companies joined Mack in producing the gasoline driven vehicles. Initially the conveyances were known as "rail motor cars" but popular usage eventually gave them the name of "rail buses."

One such Mack product was a thirty-five passenger rail bus completed on October 19, 1923, at the company's plant in Allentown, Pennsylvania. Designated "Model ACX" for its particular construction, the vehicle was proudly sent on a nation-wide tour of railroad centers in an effort to obtain orders.

The vehicle's overall length was 38'8", and it was designed for relatively long trips. Rear door en-

---

1. Three of the Mack ACX rail buses were in service as late as 1959 in Havana. A comprehensive chronicle of the vehicles can be found in "History of Mack Rail Motor Cars and Locomotives," (Lehigh Valley Chapter, National Railway Historical Society, Inc., 1959) edited by Randolph L. Kulp.

The acquisition of Locomotive No. 23 served as the occasion for California Western trainmen to pose proudly for this picture. Steam engines continued in logging service and on some passengers runs even after the CWR began using its first Skunk rail bus.

CALIFORNIA WESTERN RAILROAD

Locomotive No. 22 and its tender await a call to service in the CWR train shed. The line's equipment was turned on "Y's" rather than in a roundhouse.

trances were provided, and it included toilet facilities and a baggage compartment.

(See Appendix for engineering drawings of this vehicle and other rail buses used by the California Western.)

The price tag for the rail bus was $12,524.

This was approximately half the 1923 cost of a steam locomotive suitable for passenger service, making the gasoline-powered car something of a bargain. The vehicle not only contained its own engine but also a passenger compartment, eliminating expenditures for coaches.

Word of the Mack products reached Fort Bragg, where the California Western was seeking ways to reduce costs without cutting the passenger service that had become so much a part of the community's life. Carleton A. Curtis, CWR's general manager, went east to inspect the rail bus.

Impressed with the potential of the vehicle for service, Mr. Curtis arranged for Mack to demonstrate the rail car on the redwood route.

The little rail bus interrupted its tour of transportation centers to make the trek to Fort Bragg — where it eventually was to achieve fame. It arrived in 1925, piloted by a Mack engineer and making its way under its own power across the nation. It began to prove its worth carrying passengers on the main line to Willits.

Fort Bragg residents knew that the CWR official's trip was made to acquire new equipment, but they were unfamiliar with rail buses generally.

They were surprised, to put it mildly, when the vehicle arrived.

It looked like a cross between a bus and a streetcar without a trolley pole.

Regardless of looks, the rail bus did its job efficiently and the California Western decided to put the car into regular service. Purchase details were arranged and the transaction officially was completed on December 30, 1925.

After its purchase, the rail bus was modified from its original factory design. Its length was extended approximately eight feet and its seating capacity was reduced by five to provide more comfort for passengers.

Designated "M-80" — the letter indicating that it contained its own motive power — the rail bus went into service.

There was initial skepticism among the passengers over the practicability of the unusual vehicle.[2]

Trainmen also demonstrated reluctance over operating the rail bus. Only after some "coaxing" did the company obtain volunteers to man the vehicle.

Soon, however, passengers found the little bus quite pleasant for travel. And in the years to follow operation of the vehicle was to be a prized assignment eagerly sought by California Western trainmen.

Numerical or alphabetical designations proved

---

2. According to information supplied the author in 1963 by Amel T. Nelson, CWR auditor when the rail bus was acquired and later the railroad's vice president and general manager.

inadequate. The little rail car obviously had its own personality.

Amused yet pleased residents tried many nicknames on the arrival. Borrowing from the era's automotive slang, the M-80 was the "puddle jumper" or "Tin Lizzy." Noting a newspaper comic section favorite, some riders called the rail bus "Barney Google."

Other passengers jokingly dubbed the vehicle the "Galloping Goose."

None of the names seemed to fit. Finally, the car was unceremoniously christened "The Skunk" — a nickname that was to bring fame to the California Western.

How precisely the name originated and what imaginative soul concocted the famous monicker appears lost in history.

One story maintained that youngsters watching the rail bus with fascination likened the vehicle to a skunk because of the engine jutting outward like the nose of an animal.

The most popular version holds that veteran trainmen were familiar with steam locomotives and re-

marked on the odor of the fumes from the gasoline engine.

This aroma, they declared, was no better than that of a skunk.

It mattered little how or why the name was provided: when people referred to the M-80, they began to speak of it as "The Skunk."

Trainmen led the way in labeling the rail car "Skunk" when they spoke of the M-80. Passengers relied on its numerous other nicknames for many years. It was not until the mid-1930's that the CWR employees' jargon for the rail bus filtered down to popular usage with the public.

CWR officials reportedly first resented such an undignified nickname for the equipment. They noted quite correctly that the little car faithfully was doing an efficient job formerly performed by a locomotive, tender, and two coaches.

Any resentment over importing the unusual equipment soon vanished. The affectionate nickname became semi-official as the rail bus went about its task of hauling passengers through the redwoods.

The smokestack of Locomotive No. 22 wears a protective cap to guard against forest fires while operating.

The S. S. Brunswick, a 512 ton vessel that flew the flag of Union Lumber's National Steamship Company, was pictured in 1904 at harbor of Fort Bragg.

10.   And Ships, Too

Ships joined the Iron Horse in building a logging kingdom in the redwoods along the Mendocino Coast.

The Union Lumber Company's incorporation of the National Steamship Company in 1901 emphasized its initial dependence on the Pacific Ocean to carry redwood to the markets of San Francisco and beyond. Prior to creation of its nautical arm, Union relied on contracts with other shipping firms. Its own naviga-

tion company assured not only economical but ready ship service.

Eight ships flew the National flag during the company's lifetime. Some met doom on the rocky Mendocino coast.

First ship of the National fleet was the 512-ton *Brunswick*, built in North Bend, Oregon, in 1898 and purchased five years later by Union.

The *National City*, a 310-ton vessel built in 1888

at San Francisco, was acquired in 1906 — just in time to help during the earthquake.

The year 1908 brought acquisition of two vessels, the 415-ton *Coquille River,* built in 1896, and the *Arctic,* constructed in 1901.

Three ships christened *Noyo* flew the National banner at varying times. The company's eighth ship was the gas schooner *Coquell.*

Three of the vessels met tragic ends in the swirling, treacherous currents off Point Arena on the Mendocino coast. The company's first *Noyo,* a 316-ton vessel, was wrecked in 1914. The 392-ton *Arctic* met its end in the rocky waters eight years later. The second *Noyo,* a 1,419 steam schooner purchased in 1923, was wrecked in 1935.

The Union Lumber Company gradually stepped out of the maritime industry. The *Brunswick* was sold in 1931 to the Hammond Lumber Company and the *National City* was acquired in 1918 by Peru.

The last ship to fly the National flag was the third *Noyo,* a 1,484-ton ship purchased in 1935 and sold five years later to Thailand.

There was a mariner's touch, of course, in the rails, too. The Iron Horses rolled to the redwoods from the Pacific under the official name of the California-Western Railroad and Navigation Company.

While the railroad's articles of incorporation permitted it to operate ships, the company never entered this field. The rail line did own the wharf at Soldiers Harbor and had jurisdiction over loading of the ships.

As less reliance went to maritime activities and more was placed on the rails, the suffix "and navigation company" was dropped from the CWR's corporate title. The change became official on January 1, 1948.

The Iron Horse — and the Skunk — rather than ships reigned supreme for transportation.

The S. S. Noyo, first National steamship vessel to bear the name, awaits a cargo on the rocky coast.

UNION LUMBER COMPANY COLLECTION

11. *The Skunk Has Brothers*

The Great Depression of the 1930's brought grim days to the redwood kingdom as it did to other parts of the nation. Commerce slowed and there was little construction. Fewer shipments of logs rolled over the California Western and few passengers rode the Skunk. Most people had no place to go and little money with which to go.

The CWR's gross revenues, ranging from $212,-000 to $300,000 during the 1920's, toppled to $120,-000 in 1932. More than one hundred people were on the railroad's payroll during the twenties; just seventy-one were at work in 1933.

The railroad managed to keep its books in the profit column during most of the Depression. Yet profits of $4,146 in 1934 and $3,767 in 1935 amounted to poor returns on an investment valued at $2 million.

Profits would have been much less, if present at all, had it not been for the faithful Skunk operating instead of a more costly locomotive with its coaches.

The Skunk proved quite acceptable to passengers.

Moreover, it was relatively easy to operate. A battery-powered self starter turned over the engine and the gears shifted like those of an automobile. The engineer regulated the speed while the tracks took care of the steering.

While the Skunk served as the main reliance for riders between Fort Bragg and Willits, steam locomotives still performed limited passenger duty. Coaches "42" and "43," acquired in 1908 and used on the premiere trip when the line was completed in 1911, faithfully followed the Iron Horses for passenger duty.

The Skunk, however, was most economical for passenger service. When the opportunity presented itself in 1934 for acquiring a second rail bus, the California Western obtained another member of its Skunk family.

The addition came from the Morehead and North Fork Railroad of Morehead, Kentucky. The firm was using a forty-one passenger rail bus built in 1926 by the Edwards Railway Motor Car Company

Here is the way Skunk M-100 looked while serving passengers on the Morehead and North Fork Railroad in North Carolina. The car was remodeled for CWR service.

A. E. BARKER COLLECTION

Skunks M-200 and M-80 meet at Northspur, almost midway between Fort Bragg and Willits. The efficient service of the rail buses prompted the California Western to add to their ranks as the years passed.

of Sanford, North Carolina. When passenger traffic toppled, the Kentucky firm decided to dispose of the rail car.

When introducing its product in 1924, Edwards had announced it "achieved the ideal self-propelled railway car." The Edwards product acquired by the California Western boasted not one but two Buda four cylinder engines, each with sixty horsepower. Slightly larger than the M-80, it was a half inch short of forty-three feet long.

(See Appendix for reproduction of an Edwards publication giving engineering details of this rail bus.)

The California Western rebuilt the coach so it would comfortably seat thirty-six passengers instead of the forty-one for which it originally was designed.

The addition received the designation "M-100," but of course shared the "Skunk" nickname with the M-80.

The second Skunk immediately was accepted by CWR's clientele, now accustomed to rail bus travel instead of the traditional locomotives and coaches.

The new vehicle was welcome because it permitted continued use of rail bus transportation when the M-80 went to the railroad shops for maintenance.

The beauty of the redwoods continued to lure

vacationists to Fort Bragg despite the Depression, although business was anything but booming. Travelers on the railroad had declined from 16,824 in 1929 to just 8,772 in 1932. This was less than half the number of people who had ridden the redwood route in 1918.

Passenger revenue dived, too. In 1926 travelers paid $26,516 to ride the California Western, but California Railroad Commission reports for 1932 showed tickets brought only $8,149 in revenue to the company.

The reported passenger volume skyrocketed in 1933, with 18,464 — more than double the number in 1932 — riding the CWR. However, the 1933 revenue from passengers totalled only $9,078 — just $929 more than the year before. The increase in riders is credited to more logging in areas where the workers (riding on special reduced rate tickets) could be transported more easily by rails.

Even though more people were traveling by automobiles and rail passenger service was having its ups and downs, the California Western obviously was committed to using rail buses to carry those relying on its line.

A third member of the Skunk family was acquired in 1941. The addition was built in 1927 by the Skagit Iron and Steel Works of Sedro-Woolley, Washington, for the Longview, Portland, and Northern Railroad in Oregon. It subsequently was purchased by the Trona Railway, serving the Mojave Desert. Like other rural railroads, the Trona suffered costly declines in passenger traffic and sought to abandon this service.

The new arrival, designated the M-200, indeed was a giant when compared to the first two Skunks. It weighed 46,000 pounds — nearly twice as much as the M-80 — and could carry fifty-five passengers.

Reaching the California Western, the Skagit product automatically became a Skunk — a nickname that was becoming more and more affectionately attached to the line's passenger equipment with passing of the years.

While the fleet of Skunks multiplied, the California Western by no means neglected its steam power or freight cars. The engines continued to haul redwood and other freight while the Skunks served passengers.

The CWR listed a variety of rolling equipment among its freight cars. In 1912 the California Railroad Commission credited the line with having a

This is Skunk M-200 as it appeared while operating on the Trona Railway in California's Mojave Desert.

Skunk M-200 awaits passengers beneath the canopy (later removed) at the Fort Bragg depot shortly after beginning CWR service. For a picture of Skunk M-80 climbing a famous CWR curved grade, turn the page.

A. E. BARKER COLLECTION

PHOTOGRAPH PAGE FOLLOWING:
CALIFORNIA WESTERN COLLECTION

grand total of 199 cars in freight service. Topping the list were 156 flat cars (used for hauling logs as well as finished wood). The line also had three box cars, six tank cars, and a stock car.

Substantially the same amount of equipment remained on the California Western's roster until the middle of the 1920's, when it began retiring and selling freight cars. Through the 1930's, the company maintained 54 freight cars. Most of this equipment was sold in the 1940's, and the CWR began relying on freight cars leased from major railroads.

The California Western's 1961 financial report showed six freight cars and five miscellaneous pieces of rolling equipment on the roster.

The two initial locomotives acquired by the railroad were sold before the CWR tracks reached Willits. Other engines took their places and over the years locomotives were retired or acquired as needs developed.

The California Western owned twenty steam locomotives before converting to diesel. Iron Horses from the Baldwin Locomotive Works obviously were highly favored on the line, for all but five of the CWR's engines came from that company. *(See Appendix for roster of locomotives.)*

The numerical designation "13" was conspiciously absent from the roster, probably to placate the superstitions of passengers as well as railroad employees.

The CWR began 1910 with five locomotives. During the ensuing decade it sold three engines, scrapped two, and purchased six. Beginning 1920 with six engines, the company scrapped two locomotives and bought four, ending the decade with eight Iron Horses.

The 1930's saw the California Western sell one locomotive, scrap two, and purchase one engine. There were six locomotives on the CWR roster at the start of 1940; during the decade the company acquired two engines and scrapped two.

Although seven steam locomotives remained in service in 1950, their days obviously were numbered.

They soon were to be replaced by diesel locomotives, those distant relatives of the Skunk motorized rail buses.

These CWR freight cars, with wooden bodies, were photographed shortly after being rebuilt in 1923.

CALIFORNIA WESTERN RAILROAD COLLECTION

This 1910 Union Lumber farm nourished eucalyptus trees as well as young redwoods for conservation.

12. The Redwoods Grow Again

The birth of the twentieth century brought demands for forest conservation by legions of reformers typified in the personage of President Theodore Roosevelt. The redwoods became highly popular targets for protective legislation becaue of their stately beauty and relatively limited numbers.

The Union Lumber Company certainly kept pace with the progressive thought and in many cases outstepped the conservationists in preserving the redwoods.

Union pioneered numerous techniques in the redwood industry. C. R. Johnson's early day use of the bandsaw permitted cleaner cutting and eliminated waste marked by more primitive methods. Matt Markkula, a Union employee, invented the logging car chock designed to hold timber securely on rail

cars. Union's innovations, all adopted by other redwood companies, included apparatus to reduce damages to the board as it was finished, tractor logging to protect timber still standing, and numerous devices to save lives and limbs.

The Union Lumber Company's greatest contribution made the redwood trees grow again.

Aware of the obvious fact that once the big redwoods were all downed the trees' majestic beauty as well as their economic use would vanish, Union began reforestation with vigor that gladdened the hearts of conservationists.

Union in 1922 started a nursery to co-ordinate replanting the redwoods. The initial project failed because of fires, rodents, and dry years.

Undaunted, Union continued experiments until

Otis Johnson, son of "C. R.," succeeded his father as president of Union Lumber in 1940. He also served as vice president of the California Western Railroad.

eventually achieving success. Eminent botanists retained by the company studied the problem. The eventual conclusion showed it was wisest to let the oldest of the redwoods stand and rely on the younger trees for logging needs. Trees were allowed to grow for reaping on farms, not unlike the cotton or wheat 'fields in other sections of the nation.

Unlike conventional crops harvested annually, the redwoods were to be reaped by future generations.

The ultimate conclusion reached held that it was more profitable to log the younger trees and let the big redwoods, so prized by tourists and conservationists, stand.

Professor Emanuel Fritz of the University of California school of Forestry reported:[1]

On the best soils — river benches and flats — second growth redwood can produce more than 100,000 board feet per acre of lumber in sixty years. This may seem strange when the old growth produced no more in many more years. The explanation is this: Our large old-growth trees have very rough tops, too rough to make merchantable lumber. Therefore, a large part of the old tree must be left in the woods. Second growth, on the other hand, has small branches and much more of the trunk can be made into logs. Furthermore, old-growth logs are often very irregular and scarred and sometimes pitted with a heart rot. These factors make the mill losses rather heavy. Young growth logs are round, smooth, and generally free from decay. Old growth also entails more falling breakage, whereas in youth growth this loss in negligible.

Union's program therefore provided for letting the redwood trees grow much the same as fruit trees do for the years ahead.

Union Lumber Company managed to flourish and expand during the years. Its holdings, totalling approximately 45,000 acres in 1907, covered 145,000 acres by 1947.[2]

Business Week Magazine in 1937 rated Union among the six biggest producers and marketers of redwood in the world; within ten years the company grew to be among the biggest three in the industry. New outlets for redwood were sought and the increased marking campaign was linked with projects to assure a continuing supply. Business Week Magazine reported:[3]

Redwood is being promoted for use in construction of cooling towers and refrigeration plants, wine tanks (California's wine industry is close by) and oil derricks. Producers have worked out a long range selective program which they follow rigidly to place the industry on a sustained yield basis and eliminate the possibilities of total destruction in 50 to 70 years. This ties in with the national lumber policy toward conservation.

---

1. Professor Fritz was quoted in the February-March-April, 1952, edition of The Noyo Chief, a publication of the Union Lumber Company.

2. Moody's Industrial Manual (Moody's Investors Service, Inc., New York), 1948.

3. Business Week, April 17, 1937. Copyright by 1937 by McGraw-Hill Publishing Co., Inc. Used with permission.

Research for even more uses for redwood was launched under C. R. Johnson's progressive leadership. In 1937 redwood panels were placed on the market; the same year saw redwood bark — previously discarded — being used for insulation.

Grades of redwood discarded in previous years went for shingles, fence pickets, fire wood, and dunnage (used as an under lay for freight on ships and railroads). Wood chips previously burned as useless became an ingredient for paper stock, roofing paper, and linoleum.

C. R. Johnson became an acknowledged leader in the redwood industry. When the National Recovery Administration legislation was enacted as a Depression measure in 1933, he represented the industry for code authority meetings.

In 1939 he resigned the presidency, stepping into semi-retirement as chairman of Union's board of directors. He began to devote more time to a monumental collection of history books in his home in San Francisco.

Early in 1940, Johnson was stricken with an illness that developed into pneumonia. He died on February 1, just thirteen days before his eighty-first birthday.

Moving into Union's presidency was his son, Otis Johnson. Born at Fort Bragg in 1887, the younger Johnson became associated with the company when twenty-three years old. Otis Johnson had worked in virtually all phases of the industry and was well equipped to follow his father's footsteps.

Union expanded its conservation program, including "selective" logging that provided for only trees of a given size to be downed. When loggers left the scene, it was difficult to detect that a tree was missing from the forest. Early day logging had seen most trees cleared from an area during operations.

A tribute to the man who directed the company's progress for so many years came with the dedication on May 19, 1951, of the C. R. Johnson Tree Farms.

The California Western was called for service to carry onlookers to the ceremonies at Redwood Lodge, 10 miles from Fort Bragg.

Redwood sales flourished during World War II and the California Western did heavier duty than ever moving timber to help with the war effort. The post-war housing boom, together with research that increased uses for redwoods, carried sales to greater heights.

Otis Johnson's reign as Union president was

Russell Johnson became president of Union Lumber in 1957. He also was named a vice president of CWR.

short-lived as compared to his father's tenure. He died July 1, 1957, at his Lake Tahoe summer home. Otis Johnson's son, Russell, became president.

Research became increasingly important for the Union Lumber Company as the years passed and produced numerous products extending the use of redwood into fields undreamed of during the early twentieth century. Many of the products were marketed under the company's "Noyo" brand, advertised internationally.

Developments during the 1960's included processing parts of redwood bark (once regarded as

Amel T. Nelson became the CWR's general manager in 1928 and retired in 1958 as firm's vice president.

time he held the position. Trumball became president again in 1908, serving in the office for four years.[1]

The pattern of organization found C. R. Johnson serving as a CWR vice president, just as his son, Otis, and grandson, Russell, did in following years.

Charles E. Wilson succeeded Trumball as president in 1912 and served until 1917, when Fred C. White was named to the office.

White's father had been a co-owner of the lumbering firm of White and Plummer and one of the original stockholders of the Union Lumber Company. Before taking the line's presidency, Fred White was superintendent of Union Lumber and active in the CWR management (including direction of the first passenger train to Willits).

Carleton A. Curtis became general manager at approximately the same time. It was in this capacity that he handled details of purchasing Mack Motor Car M-80, which achieved fame as the Skunk.

---

1. Information on the identity and tenure of California Western presidents is based on the company's files.

waste) for use in drilling oil wells. Felted bark was manufactured into pads for the fruit packing industry.

Refinements in fabricating included a completely woven redwood fence and laminated redwood beams for exposed and plank ceilings. A pre-fabricated patio was developed that could be assembled with only four bolts.

Despite logging activities being centered in Fort Bragg, the Union Lumber Company and California Western maintained headquarters in San Francisco since it was the financial center for a vast area. Both firms had offices in the Crocker Building on Market Street.

While Union Lumber directors usually sat on the CWR board, the railway remained a corporate entity. In many cases the road's president had a legal background and doubled as the line's chief counsel.

Succeeding McIntosh as president in 1906 was Frank Trumball, who held the office for a year until being replaced by C. R. Johnson — the first and only

H. H. Sanborn, who served as CWR president from 1928 to 1941, took pride in the Skunk rail cars.

Left, Locomotive No. 21 pulls the final load of logs over the CWR's Ten Mile River Branch in April, 1949, a few months before service discontinued on the line.

Charles A. Strong, an attorney and veteran Union Lumber employee, was CWR president 1943 to 1960.

F. H. Sturges, a CWR employee since 1946, became the redwood railroad's general manager in 1960.

Succeeding Curtis as general manager in 1929 was Amel T. Nelson, who began his California Western duties in 1919 as a clerk in the audit office. He set a CWR service record, holding the managerial position (and added office of vice president starting in 1943) until his retirement in 1958.

The Skunk rolled to fame while Nelson held office.

Following Nelson's retirement, J. H. Gray served briefly as general manager.

He was succeeded by F. H. Sturges, a CWR employee since 1946. He had previously served the line as trainmaster, superintendent of transportation, station agent, and dispatcher.

White vacated the CWR presidency in 1927 and was succeeded the following year by H. H. Sanborn, who as a youth worked for the Southern Pacific. He became a rate clerk for the California Railroad Commission and studied law at night. After passing the bar examination, he was named legal counsel for the Pullman Company and the Union Lumber Company.

Sanborn took pride that he could speak the language of engineers and other trainmen. Fascinated by railroads, he could identify the distinctive whistles of most major railroads.

His great pride was the Skunk and after his retirement in 1941 he frequently rode the rail bus — as well as the cabooses of CWR freight trains.

The presidency remained vacant until 1943, when it was filled by Charles A. Strong, who also had a long and rich background in railroading.

As a youth, Strong made his way from Minnesota to Oakland, California, by working on railroads. He began employment with the Union Lumber Company as an office boy and soon earned advancements. He was given a leave of absence to study law, and after passing the bar examination became an attorney for the lumber company.

When Strong retired in 1960, he was replaced by Clair W. MacLeod, also an attorney.

MacLeod, a specialist in transportation and public utility commissions, had served as California legal counsel for the Pullman Company and the General American Transportation Corporation. He also was vice president of the American Short Line Railroad Association. MacLeod also was a member of the San Francisco Bay Area Rapid Transit Commission, which launched an ambitious program to develop commuter facilities.

Replacing steam locomotives, diesel engines went into service for the CWR. These two diesels carry finished lumber and freight cars from Fort Bragg to Willits.

Uses for redwood grew with the years. This patio scene includes table, chair, fence, and planters made from redwood showing the wood's versatility.

As redwood sales soared, the CWR continued to carry logs to the mill and finished lumber to the Northwestern Pacific connection at Willits. However when logging operations expanded, there were no track extensions; instead, roads for trucks were cut through the forests to haul timber to the railroad or directly to the mill in many cases.

The company purchased two diesel locomotives in 1949, and the efficiency they brought meant an end for the age of the colorful steam engines in the redwoods.

Diesel locomotives, while not nearly as picturesque as the puffing steam engines, were considerably more efficient. The transcontinental railroads had been in the process of switching to diesels since the mid-1930's. Their arrival on the CWR tracks was inevitable.

The close of the era brought many railroad and photography fans to Fort Bragg for final pictures and sad goodbyes to the Iron Horse.

Service on the Ten Mile River branch ended in 1949, after which faithful passenger coaches "42" and "43" were retired. One coach met an inglorious end when it was burned as a training exercise for the Willits fire department. The other was destined for more glory as a display in Travel Town, an exhibition of early day rolling stock in Los Angeles' Griffith Park.

While rail service continued on the California Western main line between Fort Bragg and Willits, diesel motor trucks began serving logging needs in the Ten Mile River area.

In 1956, the CWR acquired its third diesel engine and steam locomotive 14, the last remaining, was sold.

The day of the huffing, puffing Iron Horse on the redwood route was gone — but the era of the Skunk was only beginning.

The fourth Skunk, numbered M-300, arrives on a flatcar to be overhauled for CWR service. The rail bus previously ran on Salt Lake City's Saltair route.

Clair W. MacLeod, an attorney specializing in public utility matters, became CWR president in 1960.

ED FRIETAS PHOTOGRAPH

T he demise of colorful steam locomotives might well have spelled the end for the possibility of any degree of fame for the California Western had it not been for the Skunks, serving passengers through the redwoods so faithfully since 1926.

The Skunk was virtually overlooked during the years by all but the most ardent railroad fans. The little rail buses stepped into the spotlight in record time, however, following articles in several national magazines.

Perhaps the timing of these articles was just right to lift the Skunk to fame. Almost before people knew it, America's railroad era began to vanish. Steam locomotives were relegated to a place in a museum, and railways — their transportation monopoly long gone — were cutting back on passenger service.

Yet, trains — once the great American preoccupation — still held a warm spot in the hearts of a great portion of the public.

Diesel locomotives, efficient but lacking the ornate details of their steam predecessors, could never satisfy the longing for memories of that heritage of the steel rails that welded America.

The Skunk, somehow, did manage to capture that longing. Perhaps it was because the little rail buses, akin to antiques themselves, could bring back the flavor of less tense times in more natural surroundings than modern cities where cement, packed streets, and honking horns reign.

Although the flow of articles on the Skunk in generally circulated magazines did not begin until the 1940's, the rail bus and its route attracted comment during an earlier period in at least one trainmen's publication.

Writing in the June, 1933, issue of Locomotive Engineer's Journal, published by the Brotherhood of Locomotive Engineers, W. E. Butler enthusiastically described a 1932 CWR trip in an article poetically entitled "A Railway Tunnel Through The Redwoods."

Despite departure of the CWR's steam power, the Skunk rail buses reign. Here Skunk M-100 rolls by the redwoods.

The Skunk rail cars are very much a part of life in the redwood country and serve as subjects for art classes. This water color of a Skunk crossing Pudding Creek was the work of Craig Johansen when a 10th grade student at Fort Bragg Senior High School.

Butler, a locomotive engineer for the Sonora Railway and other roads since the 1890's, spent spare time riding over short lines and describing their attractions in articles for his fellow trainmen.

He rode the Northwestern Pacific to Willits and boarded the M-80, being operated at the time by engineer Fred Goroman. Butler described the vehicle as a "Mack truck with flanged wheels."

While California Western trainmen by this time were applying the "Skunk" nickname to the little car, Butler refrained from using the title in his article. Being a veteran locomotive engineer, he no doubt feared such a reference would indicate disrespect for CWR operators.

Butler, with an engineer's sense for details, reported that the faithful and well built M-80 "has a record of having made 350,000 miles before its main bearings were examined and they showed a wear of 1/32nd of an inch."

When passengers exceeded the rail bus seating capacity, he observed, "the Mack gets a day off and one of the steam engines is used."

Butler's article likened the M-80's route through the redwoods to a "tunnel, thirty-six miles long, composed entirely of trees — where the openings are so few that the sun strikes the track in but a few places and then only when it is between the hours of 11 a.m. and 2 p.m."

Locomotive No. 22 makes the final trip up the Ten Mile River Branch in the summer of 1949, carrying logging equipment. A trucking road replaced rails.

Greatly impressed with the California Western, he wrote that the line "has packed into it more trees, tunnels, bridges, and scenic beauty than any I have met in my thousands of miles of travel.

"The ride," he wrote, "will ever remain one of the pleasant memories of my life."

His sentiments were to be echoed down through the years by scores of writers and thousands of riders.

Among the first publications to single out the Skunk route for feature treatment was Trains Magazine, a publication edited for general railroad interests. The magazine's September, 1947, issue carried an article by Squire Knowles entitled "Westward-Ho by Railcar."

The flow of a great tide of literary praises of the Skunk had started.

Increased latter-day fame came when Model Trains featured the California Western in its Sep-

tember, 1955, issue. The line also was mentioned frequently in Railroad Magazine, circulating among railway fans.

More fame for the Skunk came in the May, 1959, issue of the National Geographic Magazine, circulating internationally to a readership devoted to travel. Writer Dean Jennings, again extolling the charm and virtues of the bus on rail wheels, wrote the feature article, "The Friendly Train Called Skunk."

Sunset Magazine editors were sufficiently impressed with the Skunk trip to recommend it on several occasions. A March, 1958, article was entitled "The Skunk Goes Over the Mountain." In its March, 1963, issue the magazine suggested the rail buses for tours of the redwood country.

Countless other articles appeared in newspaper magazine sections. The immense flow of publicity would have cost hundreds of thousands of dollars—if it could have been purchased. Such expenditures were unnecessary, for the Skunk proved a natural publicity-getter.

More and more visitors from all parts of the world began planning vacations that would take them to Fort Bragg to ride the California Western.

Passenger volume soared. In 1953, 13,440 riders enjoyed the Skunk route. By 1955, as the flow of magazine articles regarding the rail buses reached more audiences, patronage climbed to 22,097 passengers. The Skunk family carried 37,624 riders in 1959 and 44,359 passengers in 1961.

When the California Western reached Willits and transcontinental connections in 1911, hope was expressed there would be a flow of residents and prosperity to the redwood kingdom. While steel highways brought unbelievable growth to many towns, such was not the case for Fort Bragg. Its population grew steadily and slowly with the years.

Ironically, after most towns ceased to depend on their railroads to support their economies, the California Western grew to be an immense drawing card for visitors to Fort Bragg. In effect, it is a second "industry" (the first being redwood logging). Picture post cards of the rail buses sell well, as do tie clasps, ash trays, and china dishes bearing the likeness of the Skunk.

While the rail buses achieved fame, the redwood route was not forgotten as latter-day acclaim came to the California Western. Railroad fans (a loose term applying to people who not only are interested in technical rail terms but also the beauty to be seen from the window of a railway coach) discovered many reminders of the glory days of the Iron Horse along the CWR right-of-way. Redwood trees, winding tracks, unusual bridges, and colorful water towers presented themselves for cherished pictures.

While the Skunk reigns on the route, there is still room for other equipment. Special trains from

Its days of passenger service ended. Coach 43 is loaded for shipment to Los Angeles' Travel Town. The coach carried the first passengers when route opened.

ED FRIETAS PHOTOGRAPH

San Francisco to Fort Bragg are scheduled on occasion, and reservations for the tours ordinarily are sold out well in advance.

The route is the most fun, of course, when one sees it through the window of a jovial Skunk.

Thanks to the Skunk, the California Western achieved the fame ordinarily reserved only for the biggest of railroads.

To those who had enjoyed the Skunk for years, it was no mystery as to why the line had won its well deserved fame.

It was quite appropriate that with the glory coming to the Skunk, more glorious colors were befitting the celebrity.

The rail buses shed their olive railroad color in the early 1940's. They were repainted with yellow bodies topped with silver roofs.

A remodeling job gave Skunk M-100 a streamlined appearance. Skunk M-200 also was given a face-lifting job.

The exterior changes were not the only improvements for the faithful rail buses. While Skunk M-80 continued on gasoline power, M-100 was converted to diesel power in 1946. A diesel engine was installed in Skunk M-200 in 1955.

Still another addition for the cars came in the spring of 1959. For years the rail buses had affectionately been nicknamed Skunks. The time was at hand to make it official.

A caricature of a skunk, smiling and wearing a conductor's cap, was added to the yellow sides of the cars.

Fame continued to spread and more newspaper and magazine articles recommended the pleasure of riding the Skunk.

Travelers to Fort Bragg unable by circumstances to take the trip at least must snap pictures of the photogenic Skunks. They usually vow to return for the glorious ride.

People like the route through the redwood kingdom, the colorful Skunks reminiscent of both trolleys

Skunk M-80 crosses an "A" frame bridge for which the line was noted. Last of these bridges was replaced in 1963 as part of a program to modernize line.

Rail Bus M-300, formerly used in Salt Lake City, joins the Skunk family for passenger service in 1963.

Pride after the installation of a diesel engine in the Skunk prompted placement of this advertisement.

and trains, and perhaps as much as anything, the CWR personnel.

Engineers happily pull the rail buses to stops for tired hikers waving for rides, regardless of the point route. Conductors obligingly pick up groceries, newspapers, or medicines and deliver them as directed along the way. Crew members even contact doctors for emergency cases on the line.

It seems as though everyone falls in love with the Skunk.

The CWR had been rightfully happy to boast there had never been an injury accident involving a passenger car on its line. The proud record was broken on August 19, 1959, when Skunk M-80 collided with a truck crossing the tracks at Willits.

It should be noted that the mishap occurred out of the Skunk's native habitat of tracks and quiet redwoods on a busy highway.

All passengers escaped death, but ten were injured and the Skunk was damaged so severely that it was not returned to duty until April, 1960. Skunks

M-100 and M-200 took over passenger runs during the interval.

Even on its freight operations the California Western built up a proud safety record during the years despite floods and landslides, thanks to strict adherence to safety regulations. California Railroad Commission reports year after year credited the line with not even having minor mishaps. One of the few tragic accidents came on January 11, 1936, when Engine 23 crashed through a trestle that, unknown to the trainmen, was damaged. Bill King, the engineer, survived, but the fireman, Herman Gustafson, was killed.

The California Western's most publicized accident occurred September 26, 1964, when Skunks M-80 and M-100 were involved in a head-on crash 14½ miles east of Fort Bragg. An investigation indicated that one of the rail cars over-ran the meeting place on the line.

Most of the 73 passengers on the two cars suffered injuries and the incident commanded considerable attention nationally in newspapers and over

Pride after the installation of a diesel engine in the Skunk prompted placement of this advertisement.

television because of the fame the CWR had attained.

Skunk M-80 was virtually destroyed as a result of the impact and CWR officials — although urged to do so by rail fans — debated over whether to rebuild the vehicle because of the high cost involved.

Immediately after the accident, California Western officials placed even more emphasis on safety, reassuring prospective passengers that precautions had been taken to prevent a reoccurrence of such an incident.

As the years passed and word of the Skunks spread by personal recommendation and an increasing volume of newspaper and magazine stories, schedules were expanded to accommodate the crowds.

The once proud Northwestern Pacific line long ago ended its daily passenger trains through Willits.

Other railroads were cutting back their service as passenger volume sank lower and lower.

But not the CWR.

Fashioned from flowers, this float in a Willits parade depicted Skunk M-80 — indicating the fame that was growing for the picturesque rail buses.

Boy Scouts arrive at a camp aboard a Skunk rail bus that helped make their outing even more memorable.

JAMES GAYNER COLLECTION

In 1963 the California Western purchased the fourth member of its Skunk family. The addition was rescued from oblivion after passenger service was abandoned on the Salt Lake, Garfield, and Western Railway's Saltair line.

The addition, built in 1935 by the American Car and Foundry Company, previously served passengers on North Carolina's Aberdeen and Rockfish Railroad Company. The line connected with the Cape Fear Railroad to Fort Bragg, North Carolina — named for the same Braxton Bragg honored by the California Fort Bragg where the rail bus was to resume service.

The new rail bus, biggest of all on the CWR, weighed 52,060 pounds. It was built to seat fifty-seven passengers, or nearly double the riders accommodated on the M-80 that pioneered the line's Skunk service.

A sign of the time when it was built and the area it was designed initially to serve showed on the builder's plans. Specifications defined the seating capacity as "thirty-eight white" plus "nineteen colored" passengers. The dividing line was near the rail bus center by its two toilet compartments.

There was no segregation, of course, on the jovial Skunk line where everyone shared in the enjoyment of the redwoods and the additional rail bus would provide service for the growing number of people riding the CWR.

The M-80 retained gasoline power during its years of service. The other Skunks were improved Cummins diesel engines (installed by Watson and Meehan of San Francisco). The M-100 received a 150 horsepower engine in 1946 and a 165 horsepower diesel went into the M-200 in 1955.

While being rebuilt for California Western service, the fourth rail bus was equipped with a 220 horsepower diesel engine — a substantial improvement over the 168 horsepower gasoline engine provided by the factory.

The rebuilding also saw the seating capacity of the new rail bus increased to sixty-five passengers from the fifty-seven for which it was originally designed.

The new Skunk — for every CWR passenger car is designated Skunk — was numbered the M-300 and entered service in 1963.

Obviously, the glory days of the Skunk were just beginning even though they had passed for most railroads.

This model of Skunk M-80 was produced in HO
scale and proved a popular item in hobby shops.

14. *Modeling the California Western*

As the fame of the California Western spread
among railway history fans and the general public,
the Skunk line attracted devotees among another
group — the model railroaders.

Charming in real life, the CWR became a fascinating railroad to model in miniature for a number
of logical reasons.

Model railroading grew rapidly following World
War II. In the early days, the proverbial joke evolved
regarding dad's appropriations of junior's Christmas
train. Model railroading made no secret of the fact
that the hobby was intended particularly for adults.

Unlike the traditional toy electric train boxed
and ready for operation, the hobby of model trains

became an avocation demanding a variety of technical
and artistic skills.

A better name for the hobby might be "miniature
trains," for in effect the dedicated hobbyist operates
a small railroad. Large layouts frequently call for
several operators, who are assigned duties in keeping
with the nomenclature of real railways. Trains roll
at scale speeds, often on "schedules," and railroad
safety rules reign.

Factory manufactured scale models, meticulously
and beautifully detailed, form the nucleus of most
layouts. Models of locomotives, passenger coaches,
freight cars, and depots from a famous-name railroad ordinarily give identity to the scale operation.

107

A miniature railway scene (in H0 gauge scale) built by Hank Johnston features minutely detailed reproductions of logging activities. Below, a scene on the CWR's Ten Mile River Branch is ideal for modeling.

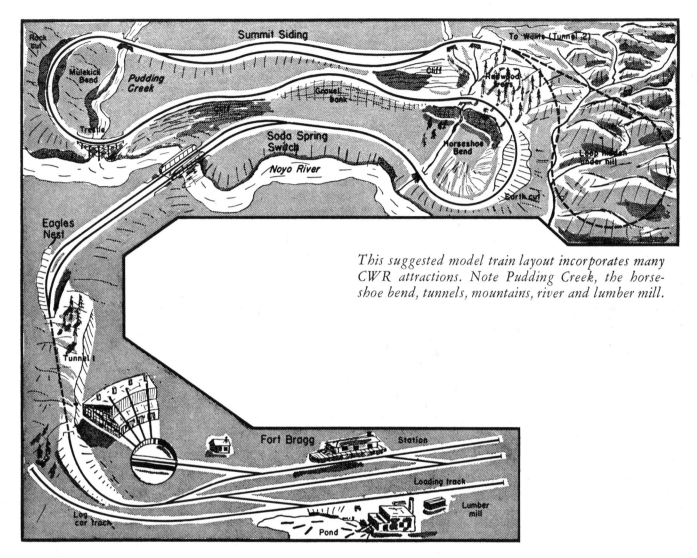

This suggested model train layout incorporates many CWR attractions. Note Pudding Creek, the horseshoe bend, tunnels, mountains, river and lumber mill.

Eventually, however, seasoned and serious modelers depart from the standards as they yearn to build unusual rail equipment and layouts. Obtaining measurements and other specifications of the rolling stock of lesser known but frequently more picturesque railroads, hobbyists build scale prototypes with materials available at model shops.

Miniature railroading thus permits its devotees to follow and develop numerous skills. These include basic mechanical proficiency in assembly, the more refined techniques of painstaking detail work, and a know-how of electricity for wiring the two rail track and operating signals. In addition, the hobby demands the artistic touch needed to develop and build authentic scenery adding the final bit of realism to a layout. Finally, and perhaps most important, it requires imagination to coordinate the many skills and use them in adapting layouts permitting use of varied equipment.

Needless to say, the use of these numerous skills is an excellent means of reducing the tensions of daily life by providing interests and outlets ordinarily not available to most people.

Scale modeling certainly is not limited to men and older boys. Many wives, daughters, sisters, and mothers join in the fun by painstakingly building detailed scenery adding authenticity to layouts.

Perfection of these modeling arts and skills to varying degrees spurs hobbyists seeking new challenges by utilizing the equipment of the more picturesque short lines of American railroading.

The California Western takes its place among the most fascinating of the nation's railways in suggesting numerous imaginative layouts for the scale fan.

First, the Skunk rail bus permits the use of a most unusual piece of rolling equipment. By its very nature it is picturesque and so distinguished in appearance that the Skunk is scenery in itself. The rail bus is a train in itself without need of a locomotive and coaches.

On a line such as the CWR it is the logical piece of equipment to carry passengers on short hauls.

Many modelers have taken it upon themselves to assemble miscellaneous parts in order to build prototypes of the faithful Skunk that adds distinctiveness to their layouts.

So popular did the California Western become that a Los Angeles area firm produced a scale prototype of Skunk M-80, using detailed drawings of the real rail car. The realistic reproduction proved highly popular with miniature railroaders.

A prototype of the picturesque rail car indeed can add color to a model railroad layout.

The Skunk, of course, is only one of many attractions the CWR holds for imaginative modelers.

The railroad at varying times owned twenty steam locomotives, including small switchers, a logging Shay, and big ten-wheeler engines. The variety of equipment presents numerous modeling opportunities.

Modern equipment is in order with a California Western layout since the line began using diesel engines in 1949.

Other interesting rolling equipment is in order because of the CWR passenger and combination coaches as well as the logging, gravel, and redwood chip cars.

The railroad's "A" frame bridges, differing from the conventional by obtaining overhead support to avoid damage by logs, can help create unusual scenery.

The mountain terrain distinguishing the road's route offers opportunities galore for hobbyists specializing in scenery. The timber products also permit the construction of picturesque logging inclines down the mountain slopes to rail sidings.

The California Western's connections at the Soldiers Harbor wharf offers many possibilities for those wishing to add a marine setting to their layouts.

The railroad's winding tracks, in many cases in proximity at varied elevations because of the steep grades, enable modelers building in cramped quarters to use considerable lengths of trackage.

Much scenery development is afforded by the small stations and colorful water towers of redwood along the CWR route. Other scenery suggestions come from the numerous picturesque structures of redwood that distinguished Fort Bragg even in the 1960's.

The two tunnels in the wooded mountains are naturals for any miniature railroad layout.

And not to be forgotten are the majestic redwoods, scale models of which can add grandeur to any scene.

The California Western indeed was heaped with ideas to produce more fun in model railroading.

Suggested model track layout plans based on the California Western were featured in the September, 1955, issue of Model Trains, published by the Kalmbach Publishing Company of Racine, Wisconsin. Numerous articles and photographs recommending the CWR as a line to model have been featured in Model Railroader, monthly magazine also published by Kalmbach.

"It's a honey, all right," advised Andy Anderson, author of the Model Trains article, "and it lends itself to modeling either as a steam pike, as in the old days, or as a diesel road as now. What's more, its operating men are as chummy as model trainmen, and that is enough to make it the most!"[1]

Anderson then offered advice that would bring knowing nods from those who have ridden the Skunk.

"The main thing you'll need to be in keeping is something you can't buy at a hobby shop or build from a kit," he wrote, "yet is very easy to come by."

"That's the spirit of friendliness, of neighborliness," he explained, "that follows the CWR all the way from Willits to Fort Bragg."

---

1. Andy Anderson, "The California Western:: A Railroad You Can Model," Model Trains, September, 1955, Pp. 28-31. Copyright by Kalmbach Publishing Company; excerpts used with permission.

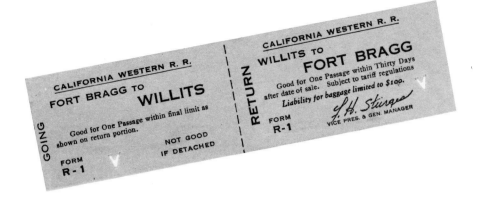

15. You Ride The Skunk

The day has arrived when you're finally going to take a long anticipated trip in the Skunk.

Typical of most visitors, you probably arrived in Fort Bragg the day before, reserved a hotel or motel unit for the night, and purchased a ticket for the next day's trip so as to be certain of a seat.

The Fort Bragg-Willits round-trip fare is $3.45, a bargain in comparison to the $4.50 charged on opening of the line on 1912 — a time when a dollar was much more difficult to earn.[1]

The rules ban standing in the aisles of the Skunk and tickets are sold only for the available seats. All of the rail buses go into operation on busy days to avoid disappointments. Additional departures are provided from June through September, the most pleasant months in the redwoods and consequently the period when the crowds arrive.

Highways have been carved up the Mendocino coast and through its mountains.

But the rail era still glows brightly at Fort Bragg, where the faithful Skunks await.

You approach the depot at the foot of Laurel Avenue. Greeting you from atop the building is a caricature of a saucy Skunk saluting you and all other rail fans.

It's not quite time for the Skunk to load passengers and the tracks are empty except for box cars,

---

1. Fares of $3.45 for the round-trip or $2.30 for one-way trips became effective July 1, 1956. Immediately prior to that time the one-way fare was $2.30 but three types of round-trip tickets were sold: those valid for three days cost $2.60, one to be used within 21 days sold for $3.10, and a ticket usable for three months was priced at $3.75. The tickets with the longer expiration periods were intended for persons residing in the forests or making longer trips from Fort Bragg.

Travelers gather around the Skunk rail bus at the Fort Bragg depot as departure time approaches.

WATSON AND MEEHAN COLLECTION

A smiling Skunk symbolizing the rail bus service is perched atop the CWR depot in Fort Bragg.

Remaining from the steam engine era, redwood water towers add a picturesque touch to the CWR route.

their tops removed to allow filling with redwood chips bound for pulp mills, and a caboose.

The waiting passengers admire the caboose, similar to that of most railroads except for its coat of striking yellow paint.

There's a murmur from the crowd. The Skunk has left the engine house. Its bell ringing happily, the rail bus moves up from the yards. As it approaches, you see that this particular Skunk is the M-100, the Edwards product acquired by the CWR in 1934.

The crowd watches expectantly as the Skunk maneuvers through switches and backs into the depot area, coming to a stop.

The conductor is King O. Nelson.

Wearing a red vest beneath his uniform, he steps from the stairs. He smiles at the crowd.

"All aboard," he says, and the ring of his voice has all of the enthusiasm of one inviting passengers to step onto a train about to make a transcontinental trip.

You're fortunate enough to find a seat up by engineer John Galliani, who explains he's a comparative newcomer to the CWR.

"I started in 1917," Galliani says. His first CWR assignments were as a brakeman and conductor. He began operating the Skunk over its 40-mile route in 1936.

"And I never make a trip but what I don't see something new and wonderful," he adds. "I wouldn't trade my job for any other in the world."

Galliani's experience during a night-time ride on the Skunk with a corpse has earned him fame on his own right and the almost legendary story has been told in many magazine articles describing the CWR.

Galliani was engineer for a run leaving Willits at 3 a.m. The front compartment was so filled with express that no one could reach the motorman's cab. The freight included a body bound to a Fort Bragg undertaker.

"As we slid into the tunnel at the summit," Galliani recalled, "I heard a grunting. It seemed to come from that big box. I was scared. Every time we swung around a curve, I heard a grunt.

"The express cut me off from the rest of the crew," he continued, "so the only thing I could do was keep the Skunk rolling to Fort Bragg. When we arrived it was a cold night but I was sweating."

The corpse was unloaded but the grunting continued.

Galliani peeked into another crate and there was

Engineer John Galliani and conductor King O. Nelson check rolling order before the Skunk departs. Below, Nelson throws switch to clear way for car.

a little pig. Mad at himself for being frightened, he tossed the crate to the ground. The crate broke and the pig scampered away.

"And I sure had a heck of a time catching him," Galliani recalled.

Your trip on the Skunk obviously will be more pleasant. The season is spring and the day is bright and sunny. Virtually every seat on Skunk M-100 is filled. It is evident from the people remaining on the platform that a second Skunk will be operating to accommodate the crowds.

At promptly 9:45 a.m. **Nelson** calls a final "all aboard" and the Skunk pulls out, its bell ringing gaily. Galliani sounds the air horn, warning motorists on U. S. Highway that the Skunk will cross the artery. You see riders in automobiles pointing and smiling at the yellow and silver rail bus. Probably some will park their cars in Fort Bragg and buy tickets for a ride on the rails.

The Skunk glides past a siding where more freight cars loaded with chips have been spotted. On the left is the cemetery, resting place of many loggers and railroaders. Pine trees, intermixed with redwoods, appear along the right-of-way. The tracks begin to climb. The trip to Willits is well under way.

113

The rail bus rounds a bend: here is Pudding Creek. Redwood trees rise in splendor along the banks; ferns drape down to the edge of the railroad right-of-way. You imagine how busy the area must have been at the turn of the century when redwood logging centered in the area. Lumberjacks arrived on the Iron Horse from Fort Bragg, breaking the still of the forest with humming saws. Today the woods again are tranquil. But ahead of you is a quartet of youthful fishermen trying their luck from a vantage point near the right-of-way. They hear the air horn, see the Skunk coming, and move to safety. They wave as the rail bus passes; even their little dog seems to be smiling at the Skunk.

Pudding Creek, just a mile from Fort Bragg, is the area where loggers and their wives or girl friends came for Sunday outings via the California Western during the railroad's early days. It is as beautiful as ever.

You move your eyes briefly from the scenery and look at the other passengers. Everyone seems satisfied: the scenery could never be duplicated, and the Skunk is as much fun to ride as legend had it.

Alongside the track is a deserted roadbed. This is Glen Blair Junction, 3.5 miles from Fort Bragg. It was from this point that the Glen Blair Lumber Company's rail line stretched more than four miles northward through the redwoods to Smith Creek.

Rounding a curve, the Skunk spans Pudding Creek and heads into Tunnel No. 1, dug by the Chinese. The interior is supported by sturdy redwood timber.

The tunnel carries the railroad through the mountain to the Noyo River, whose canyon the tracks follow for approximately 18 miles of the push to Willits. The sparkling waters gush over rocks, merrily making their way to the Pacific south of Fort Bragg. You see more fishermen casting for trout.

"Wonder if they're biting today?" Galliani asks, peering down at the sportsmen. "I'm going to have to find out and come up here on a day off."

The Skunk curves with the river, and each turn unfolds new beauty of towering redwoods, giant ferns, and patches of wildflowers. The river is on your right for a moment, and then, as the tracks span the waters, on your left. To one side of the right-of-

Skunk M-100 rolls through the redwood country. The cars travel at maximum speed of 45 miles an hour.

Comfortably seated aboard the Skunk, passengers of all ages enjoy the beautiful scenery of the redwoods.

way you see an abandoned bridge left standing after engineers straightened the track as part of the program to improve the railroad.

The original 115 bridges have been reduced to 32 as the result of constant improvement, and lighter rail has been replaced with 110 and 112 pound rail that would do credit to a major railroad.

Looking up ahead on the right-of-way, you see a deer on the tracks. Few automobiles and trucks penetrate the area, and the Skunk is among the few vehicles that enters his wooded paradise. The deer takes a frightened look at the approaching rail bus and scampers into his redwood kingdom.

Galliani blows the air horn: the Skunk is approaching South Fork, at the 6.6 mile post from Fort Bragg. Waiting vacationists will step from the shaded station to join the trip. This is the point where the south fork of the Noyo River flows into the main branch.

The Skunk picks up a fisherman, rod in hand, and rolls again. Alongside the main right-of-way is a siding by a gravel deposit. CWR gravel cars stand to be loaded and taken to points where new ballast is being placed with track improvements.

Here and there along the right-of-way you see water tanks, supported by heavy redwood posts. These are picturesque reminders of the days when

the Iron Horses rolled the route, stopping to quench the thirst of their boilers.

Suddenly the redwoods give way to a beautiful green meadow. A flock of sheep grazes idly in the grass, growing excellent wool in this higher, cooler elevation. Nearby is an apple orchard. The crisp air helps to produce delicious fruit on the trees.

Ahead on the tracks is a crouching cat, ready to pounce on a bird. He is startled by the approaching Skunk and races through the waving grass directly to a hole beneath a cabin's foundation. You make a bet to yourself that the cat's sure-fire knowledge of exactly where he can find refuge means that the rail bus interruption is almost a daily occurrence for him.

The air horn breaks the stillness again to signal the Skunk's approach to a station. The rail bus pulls into Redwood Lodge, where the station with its pillars of squared redwood timber reminds you of a miniature Grecian temple.

The lodge giving the stop its name burned in 1963 after having long been an attraction for vacationists. Surrounding the area is the C. R. Johnson Tree Farm.

Rolling again through the redwoods, the Skunk rounds a bend — and whoa!

Planted squarely on the track is a man in hiking shorts placidly taking motion pictures of the ap-

115

proaching train. His serenity makes you wonder if he expects a giant crane to lift him from danger just in time

"Look at that fellow," grins Galliani, easing the throttle and letting the Skunk brake with its own gears. "He's got faith. Do you suppose he thinks we're going to stop?"

The cameraman evidently has his doubts, although he feels the scene is too good to miss. He continues to take pictures as the car draws nearer, but the camera shakes as though he may be wondering if these will be his last pictures.

Galliani is slowly applying his brakes.

"Let him get a good picture," he says.

The cameraman jumps from the track.

"He didn't trust us," the engineer laughs. The Skunk stops and the cameraman, laughing by now as he considers the story he can tell to go with his pictures, boards the Skunk.

You notice that the rail bus has been climbing while it rolls through the beautiful mountain country. The elevation at Redwood Lodge was 78 feet above sea level, and by the time the Skunk reaches Grove — just 2.6 miles farther — the altitude is 125 feet.

Residents along the route receive their supplies via the Skunk, thus saving a journey. Below, food is unloaded at a shaded station along the CWR route.

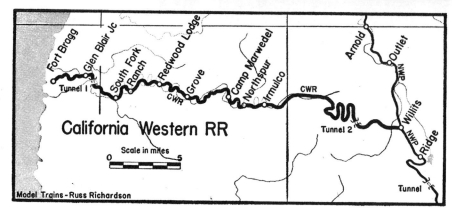

COURTESY MODEL RAILROADER MAGAZINE

The redwoods are thick and tall, and you can barely see the blue of the sky as you look upward between the giants.

Still climbing, the Skunk passes Camp Three, at the 15 mile mark and at an altitude of 125 feet, and Camp Four, a mile farther and at a 228-foot elevation. During the early days, logging camps received increasingly higher numerical designations as they were extended deeper into the forest with the rails. Logging is being concentrated in other areas and the camp designations now do little more than mark points on the route — and recall a colorful but bygone area.

Next is Alpine, 264 feet above sea level and at the 18 mile point from Fort Bragg. The railroad ended here in the early days and passengers alighted to board stagecoaches to reach Willits.

The air grows crisper while the Skunk climbs higher. The big trees tower alongside the tracks, and you must stretch your neck to see the blue sky. The tops of the redwoods nearly touch, making the route almost like a tunnel through a forest.

The rail bus passes Camp Silverado, operated by the Boy Scouts of America, and Camp Mendocino, summer outpost for the San Francisco Boys' Club. Youngsters enjoy outings in the redwoods they never will forget.

A few more twists and turns and the tracks reach Olde Camp Seven, center for logging operations during the first part of the century.

The CWR is a single track line. The cost of building double tracks through the rugged mountains would have been prohibitive, and the traffic never warranted dual sets of rails. There are side tracks at the stations — as well as at other points — so trains can pull to the side while another passes.

JAMES GAYNER COLLECTION

Here is the view from the Skunk as it travels through the redwoods.

Engineer John Galliani sits at the controls of Skunk M-100, operating the rail bus skillfully and safely— and with an affection that moves him to vow that he wouldn't trade his job for any other in the world.

Up ahead is a station unmarked on the timetable, but nevertheless a stop if someone is waiting. A sign on the little redwood shelter announces that this is "Emmett," a designation no doubt given for the owners of adjacent property.

The Skunk is a friendly train. Not content with stops at its regular stations, it pauses for hikers or fishermen signaling for rides anywhere along the route. Its crews are just as friendly, and when a cabin owner requests a loaf of bread or a newspaper, the railroaders drop off the desired item on the next trip.

One of the region's few automobile roads (a thought you'd like to forget while riding the Skunk) crosses the tracks at Irmulco. Here the river valley widens and redwoods again give way to green meadows. Apparently unaware of the passing Skunk, dairy cows nibble at the grass.

Irmulco took its name from the Irvine and Muir Lumber Company, an early day logging firm. You note that since the last station, Northspur, 2.6 miles back, the Skunk has climbed 86 feet and now is at the 408 foot elevation.

Leaving Irmulco, the Skunk hits the longest stretch on straight track on the entire route: almost a mile in length just before reaching Shake City, at the 26.8 mile point from Fort Bragg.

The Skunk has been rolling along at approximately 25 miles an hour, and you note that it is beginning to slow slightly.

"We're going to climb," Galliani announces, still wearing the cheerful smile with which he has greeted each curve. He shifts from high to third gear.

Shake City's elevation was 560 feet, and by the time the Skunk reaches Burbeck, just a mile further, the elevation is 688 feet.

There is a murmur aboard the Skunk, and everyone is looking upward. More than one hundred feet above you see a stretch of track to be reached only after twenty minutes and eight miles of travel.

You begin to understand why it took so many years to stretch the CWR tracks from Fort Bragg to Willits.

118

The right-of-way carved into the mountains looks like this to the engineer operating the Skunk.

By the time the Skunk reaches Soda Springs, two miles past Shake City, it has climbed 248 feet; the next 3.6 miles to Clare Mill carries the tracks 463 feet higher into the mountains.

Clare Mill, 30.4 miles from Fort Bragg, is at an elevation of 1,023 feet. During the next 2.2 miles, the rail bus climbs 352 feet and reaches Crowley, at the 1,375 foot level.

Looking from the window, you see mile after mile of redwoods stretching in the distance below.

You understand why John Galliani would never trade his job for any other.

The Skunk leaves the Crowley stop, 32.6 miles from Fort Bragg and 815 feet higher than Shake City. Almost directly below is the track where the Skunk rolled nearly a half hour before.

The Skunk reaches Summit, 1,740 feet above sea level and the highest point on the line. Ahead is Tunnel No. 2, bored in 1911 to conquer the mountain barrier and link Fort Bragg with the transcontinental rail lines.

The rail bus glides through the tunnel, surfaced with cement. The car moves onto a siding and Galliani sounds the air horn.

The signal is returned by another air horn, and in a few minutes Skunk M-200 rolls up the hill enroute from Willits to Fort Bragg.

You join the other passengers in waving and taking pictures of the other Skunk as it passes and disappears into the tunnel. Skunk M-100 moves off the siding, onto the main track, and begins the downward trek to Willits.

Willits is the terminus of the route from Fort Bragg. Bottom arrow indicates route traveled by the Skunk, which uses the Northwestern Pacific Tracks for the last lap. Top arrow shows location of Willits depot.

The end of the run to Willits finds engineer John Galliani relaxing while passengers have their lunches and stroll until time for the return to Fort Bragg.

The redwoods have given way to oak trees and green meadows. Sheep graze tranquilly beneath the shade of the trees.

As the Skunk continues on the downgrade, the countryside seems to be ablaze with gold. Here are solid fields of California wild poppies, the state flower, stretching like an ocean of gold.

You are pleased, more than ever, that you rode the Skunk.

Galliani again sounds the air horn. The Skunk approaches a highway, the first since leaving Fort Bragg. The passengers in the automobiles wave, wishing, no doubt, that they could park their cars and take a carefree ride on the Skunk.

The tracks lead to the Northwestern Pacific right-of-way, and the rail bus glides along the final lap to Willits.

You alight at the Northwestern Pacific's Tyrolean station, as beautiful as the day when it was dedicated in 1916.

You'll always remember the glory of the redwood trees, verdant meadows, grazing sheep and cattle, and sparkling Noyo River as only the Skunk can unveil them.

You've ridden the Skunk.

Rolling through the forest, a Skunk rail bus helps open the beauties of the redwoods to travelers.

16. A Story Still Being Written

The redwoods watched silently, as they had for centuries, while the second century of activity grew older along the Mendocino Coast.

The big trees probably were pleased that more and more people traveled to admire them from vantage points aboard the faithful, friendly little Skunks.

For the redwoods — those oldest living things on the planet — there loomed more life and usefulness as they grew in tree farms and uncut forests.

For the California Western and its family of Skunks, there would be continued cheerful service and many miles to roll as living relics of the fading rail era.

As the CWR glided toward its hundredth birthday, it evidently was to have the distinction of being among the few rail lines in America still carrying comparatively substantial numbers of passengers.

For Fort Bragg, also approaching its hundredth

anniversary, destiny seemed imminent as a metropolis of the coastal redwood kingdom just as C. R. Johnson envisioned.

California's bludgeoning growth sent settlers into the northern valleys. Studies showed that soon these regions would be covered by endless acres of houses in the fashion of development that long ago blanketed the areas around San Francisco and Los Angeles.

Fort Bragg appeared destined as the seaside capitol for these residents. Its future development most obviously would be along the lines of an art colony as picturesque as those at Carmel and Laguna Beach.

And many visitors would arrive on the Skunk.

Seated in his home not far from the California Western depot, John Pimentel — the man who came from the Azores, fell in love with the redwoods, remained, and became brakeman on the first passenger train from Fort Bragg to Willits in 1911 — looked back at the years.

His eyes thoughtful but twinkling, he recalled the first glory days of the redwoods and their railroad.

He remembered many happy faces among the passengers on that train.[1]

"They loved the redwoods," John Pimentel smiled.

"I myself have never ceased marveling at the big trees despite more than sixty years among them," he continued. "And the people who come to ride our Skunk even these days say that pictures fail to tell the story of the grandeur. One must see the redwoods to appreciate them."

What about the people who make the trek up the Mendocino Coast during all the tomorrows?

"The redwoods will still be here," John Pimentel replied. "and they will be bringing forth cries of joy, amazement, and pleasure a hundred years from now."

---

1. In a 1963 interview with the author, Mr. Pimentel recalled vivid details of not only the first through trip but also his early days at Fort Bragg. He showed photographs taken with groups of fellow lodge brothers, of which he is among the few surviving, and was able to indentify most of their names and occupations.

CALIFORNIA WESTERN RAILROAD COLLECTION

The Appendix

A.   Roster of Locomotives and Skunks

The roster of locomotives and Skunk rail cars used on the California Western Railroad is presented on the following pages. This information includes numerous details pertaining to the construction of the Skunk rail buses, since these vehicles are indeed an unusual part of railroading. The Skunks were olive green during their initial years of CWR service, but in the early 1940's were painted yellow with silver roofs.

As in the case of most short lines, the California Western has used equipment from a variety of builders to fill its needs.

Locomotives Nos. 1 and 2 were wood burners eventually converted to using oil. The other steam locomotives were oil burners.

The weights given in the roster are for the locomotive and tender in working order for Locomotives Nos. 1 through 14; those for No. 21 and thereafter are for engines only.

Data for the roster was supplied by the California Western Railroad and the Union Lumber Company.

Roster of CWR Motive Power

No. and Date Acquired	Type	Builder	Date Built	Cylinders	Drivers	Tractive Effort	Weight	Boiler Pressure	Builder No.
STEAM LOCOMOTIVES									
1 (1905)	0-4-0	Baldwin	1885	12x14	42	7,500	50,000	130	7831
2-1st (1905)	2-4-2	Baldwin	1887	12x20	42	7,560	60,000	130	8852
2-2nd (1911)	0-4-2	Baldwin	1901	17x24	50	18,000	92,700	160	18618
3 (1905)	2-4-4	Baldwin	1884	14x20	42	?	70,000		?
4 (1905)	4-4-0	Hinkley	1883	16x24	57	?	115,000		?
5 (1906)	4-6-0	Schenectady	1880	18x24	57	20,000	163,000	170	2042
6 (1908)	0-4-0	Mason	1868	14x22	48	8,000	48,000	100	245
7 (1909)	2-6-2	Baldwin	1909	15x22	44	16,000	98,000	170	33390
8 (1910)	4-6-0	Southern Pacific	1869	18x24	57	20,000	117,000	165	2002
9 (1912)	3-T Shay	Lima	1912	12x12	32	25,750	120,000	200	2547
11 (1913)	2-6-2	Baldwin	1913	15x22	44	16,000	98,000	170	39551
12 (1914)	2-6-2	Baldwin	1914	15x22	44	16,000	110,000	170	41922
14 (1938)	2-6-2	Baldwin	1924	15x24	44	18,000	108,000	180	58050
17 — No. 7 renumbered in 1924									
21 (1920)	2-6-2	Baldwin	1920	18x24	44	30,000	140,000	200	53277
22 (1921)	2-6-2	Baldwin	1921	18x24	44	30,000	140,000	200	54878
23 (1923)	2-6-2	Baldwin	1923	18x24	44	30,000	140,000	200	57553
36 (1918)	4-6-0	Baldwin	1890 (?)	19x24	44	22,000	135,000	160	9298
38 — No. 8 renumbered in 1924									
41-1st (1922)	0-6-0	Baldwin	1901	16x24	50	15,000	72,000	160	18760
41-2nd (1940)	2-8-0	Baldwin	1920	18x22	42	26,000	121,000	180	53205
44 (1944)	2-8-2	Baldwin	1930	19x24	44	32,000	158,700	190	61306
45 (1964)	2-8-2	Baldwin	1924	19x24	48	30,000	150,000	200	58045
46 (1968)	2-6-6-2 Mallet	Baldwin	1937	18x28x24	44	30,000	247,000	200	62064

No. and Date Acquired		Builder	Date Built			Tractive Effort	Weight	Horse-power	Builder No.
DIESEL LOCOMOTIVES									
51 (1949)		Baldwin	1949			50,000	200,000	750	74408
52 (1949)		Baldwin	1949			50,000	200,000	750	74409
53 (1949)		Baldwin	1956			58,750	235,000	1,000	74193
54 (1969)		Baldwin	1969			50,000	240,000	1,200	75823
55 (1970)		Baldwin	1970			57,500	240,000	1,200	76024
56 (1970)		Baldwin	1970			57,500	240,000	1,200	76105

No. and Date Acquired		Builder	Date Built				Weight	Horse-power	
RAIL BUSES									
M-80 (1925)		Mack	1923				29,000	80	
M-100 (1934)		Edwards	1925				39,000	See Notes	
M-200 (1941)		Skagit	1927				41,590	See Notes	
M-300 (1963)		American Car	1935				52,060	See Notes	

Notes to the Roster

No. 1: This locomotive was designated *Sequoia* while serving the Fort Bragg Railroad, predecessor of the California Western. The locomotive was sold in 1906 to the lumber firm of Standish and Hickey.

No. 2 (1st): Acquired from the Fort Bragg Railroad; sold in 1910 to Irvine-Muir Lumber Company.

No. 2 (2nd): Purchased in approximately 1911 from California State Belt Railroad; scrapped in 1920.

No. 3: Purchased in 1895 by the Fort Bragg Railroad; sold in 1918 to the Mendocino Lumber Company.

No. 4: Acquired from the Southern Pacific in 1904 by the Fort Bragg Railroad; scrapped in 1914.

No. 5: Acquired from the Southern Pacific of Arizona; scrapped in 1923.

No. 6: Acquired from the Santa Fe; sold in 1910.

No. 7: Renumbered "17" in 1924.

No. 8: Acquired after use by the Central Pacific and Southern Pacific; renumbered "38" in 1924.

No. 9: Scrapped in 1917.

No. 11: Scrapped in 1947.

No. 12: Scrapped in 1950.

No. 14: Purchased in 1938 from the

NO. 4

Fruit Growers Supply Company; sold in 1956.

No. 17: Scrapped in 1938.

No. 21: Sold in 1950 to Pan-American Engineering Company.

No. 22: Scrapped in 1952.

No. 23: Scrapped in 1950.

No. 36: Acquired in 1918 from Colorado Midland Railroad; sold in 1929 to Little River Redwood Company.

No. 38: Scrapped in 1942.

No. 41 (1st): Purchased in 1922 after service on the Arizona and New Mexico Railway and El Paso and Southwestern Railway; scrapped in 1937.

No. 41 (2nd): Purchased in 1940 from the Sierra Railroad; scrapped in 1950.

No. 44: Purchased in 1944 after service with the Lamm Lumber Company of Modoc, Oregon; scrapped in 1952.

No. 45: Built for the Brownlee-Olds Lumber Company of Medford, Oregon; purchased from that firm's suc-

cessor, the Medford Corporation, in 1964 and rebuilt to begin *Super Skunk* service.

No. 46: Built for Weyerhaeuser Timber Company; later used by Rayonier, Inc., at its Hoquiam, Washington, operations; purchased in 1968 from Rayonier.

No. 51: Scrapped after being damaged in a January, 1970, accident involving Locomotives 52 and 54.

No. 52: Scrapped after being damaged in a January, 1970, accident involving Locomotives 51 and 54.

No. 53: Formerly used by the United States government and acquired in 1956 through Pan-American Engineering Company.

No. 54: Built for the Wabash Railroad; scrapped after being damaged in a January, 1970, accident, involving Locomotives 51 and 52.

No. 55: Built for the McCloud River Railroad.

No. 56: Built for the McCloud River Railroad.

No. M-80: Built by Mack Trucks,

Inc., to demonstrate rail buses; retired from service after a 1964 collision with Skunk M-100.

No. M-100: Acquired from the Morehead and North Fork Railroad of Kentucky; its two Buda four-cylinder gasoline engines, each rated 60 horsepower, were replaced in 1946 with a 150-horsepower Cummins diesel engine.

No. M-200: Built for the Longview, Portland, and Northern Railway; acquired by the CWR in 1941 from the Trona Railway; its original Buda six-cylinder, 150-horsepower gasoline engine was replaced in 1955 with a 156-horsepower Cummins diesel engine.

No. M-300: Initially used on the Aberdeen and Rockfish Railroad of North Carolina; used on the Saltair Route of the Salt Lake, Garfield, and Western Railroad, which sold it to the CWR; its original six-cylinder, 168-horsepower Hall-Scott gasoline engine was replaced by a 220-horsepower Cummins diesel engine on CWR acquisition.

CALIFORNIA WESTERN RAILROAD COLLECTION

NO. 5

NO. 7 (17)

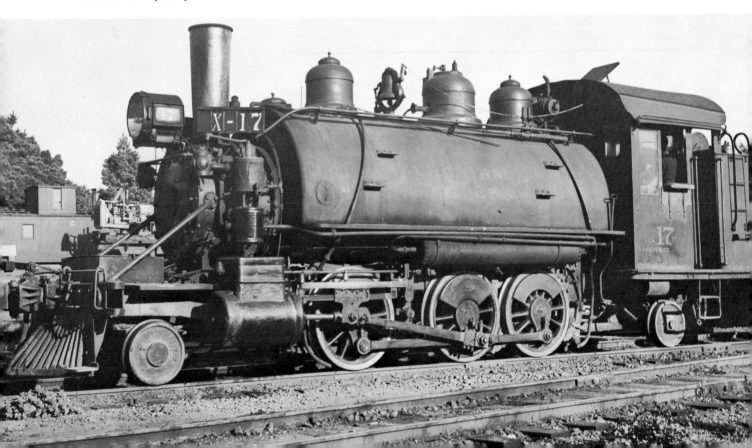

NO. 8 (38)

NO. 11

NO. 12

NO. 14

NO. 21

NO. 22

NO. 23

NO. 36

NO. 41 (2nd)

NO. 44

CALIFORNIA WESTERN RAILROAD COLLECTION

NO. 51   NO. 52   NO. 53

SKUNK M-80

Rail Motor Car M-80 was part of a series designated by its manufacturer, Mack Trucks, Inc., as Model ACX. It was first produced in 1922 and was a revision of the firm's previous Model AC initially produced in 1921. The ACX offered four rear wheels (vs. two for the AC) and an 80 horsepower engine (against 45 horsepower for the AC).

Ironically, Mack's rail bus production came to a virtual standstill after completion of the unit sold to the California Western Railroad that eventually brought fame to the cars. Producion was revived briefly in the early 1930's, but only on a limited scale.

The M-80 was completed October 19, 1923, in Mack's plant at Plainfield, New Jersey. It received serial number 60014. The vehicle was demonstrated on various railways, including the CWR where it proved its worth during 1925 trials. The railroad purchased the vehicle on December 30, 1925.

Maximum speed for the ACX was rated at 50 miles per hour. It was factory-equipped with a Mack AC four cylinder engine with a five inch bore and six inch stroke; it carried a 20 gallon gasoline tank. The engine had a gravity and splash oil system. Fuel feed was by a foot pedal. The cooling system operated with a fan drawing air that was discharged through two tubes.

The vehicle had four gear speeds each in the main (or forward) and rear transmissions. Power reached the wheels via a shaft from the engine to a bevel gear on the rear axle. The diameters of the wheels were 20 inches in front and 30 inches in the rear. The car had an air brake system. The ignition provided a high tension magneto, and the vehicle was equipped with a 12 volt generator with a matching 150 ampere Exide battery of six cells.

The rail coach's body was of pressed steel and the vehicle weighed 29,000 pounds minus passengers or cargo. The factory provided heating with a Peter Smith hot ·coal stove; ventilation came through four roof ventilators with movable louvres.

The adjoining drawings, provided by Mack, represent the California Western's vehicle except that door and seating arrangements are reversed on the M-80.

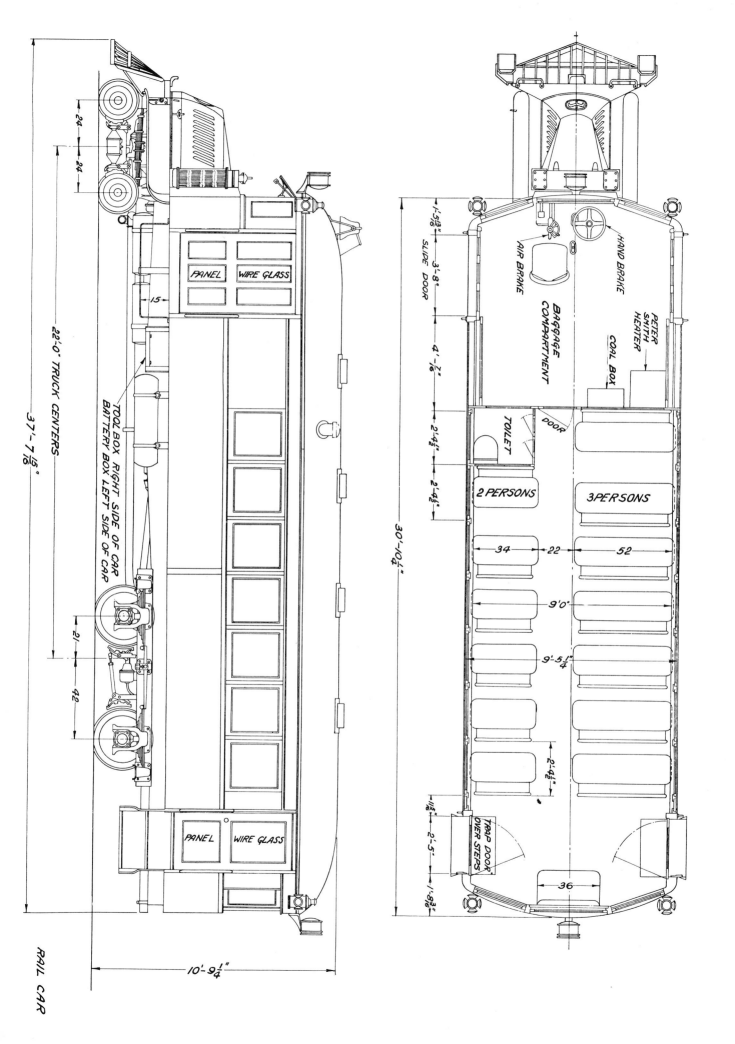

PANEL   WIRE GLASS

15

TOOL BOX RIGHT SIDE OF CAR
BATTERY BOX LEFT SIDE OF CAR

24

24

22'-0" TRUCK CENTERS

37'-7 15/16"

21

42

PANEL   WIRE GLASS

10'-9 1/4"

RAIL CAR

BAGGAGE COMPARTMENT

HAND BRAKE

AIR BRAKE

PETER SMITH HEATER

COAL BOX

DOOR

TOILET

2 PERSONS

3 PERSONS

34   22   52

9'0"

9'-5 1/4"

2'-4 1/2"

TRAP DOOR OVER STEPS

36

1'-5 3/16"

SLIDE DOOR

3'-8"

4'-7 1/16"

2'-4 1/2"

2'-4 1/2"

30'-10 1/4"

11 1/8"

2'-5"

1'-8 3/16"

SKUNK M-100

Rail Motor Car M-100 was built in 1925 by the Edwards Railway Motor Car Company of Sanford, North Carolina, and was designated Model 25.

The rail bus was equipped with two Buda four cylinder engines, each rated 60 horsepower at 1,200 r.p.m. Both engines were served by a single 65-gallon gasoline tank. The factory rated the car as capable of operating at a top speed of 60 miles per hour.

Factory specifications listed the car as having Westinghouse air brakes, 30 inch wheels, a 240-watt headlight, and a Peter Smith hot air heater. The rail car weighed 39,000 pounds and was equipped by the factory to seat 41 passengers.

The M-100 served the Morehead and North Fork Railroad of Kentucky until 1934, when it was purchased by the California Western Railroad. The car was rebuilt by the CWR prior to entering service. A 150-horsepower Cummins diesel engine was installed in the rail bus in 1946 by Watson and Meehan of San Francisco.

The adjoining manufacturer's drawings are from the collection of A. E. Barker.

See Appendix "B" for a reproduction of the 1924 Edwards Railway Motor Car Company catalog listing other details of this vehicle.

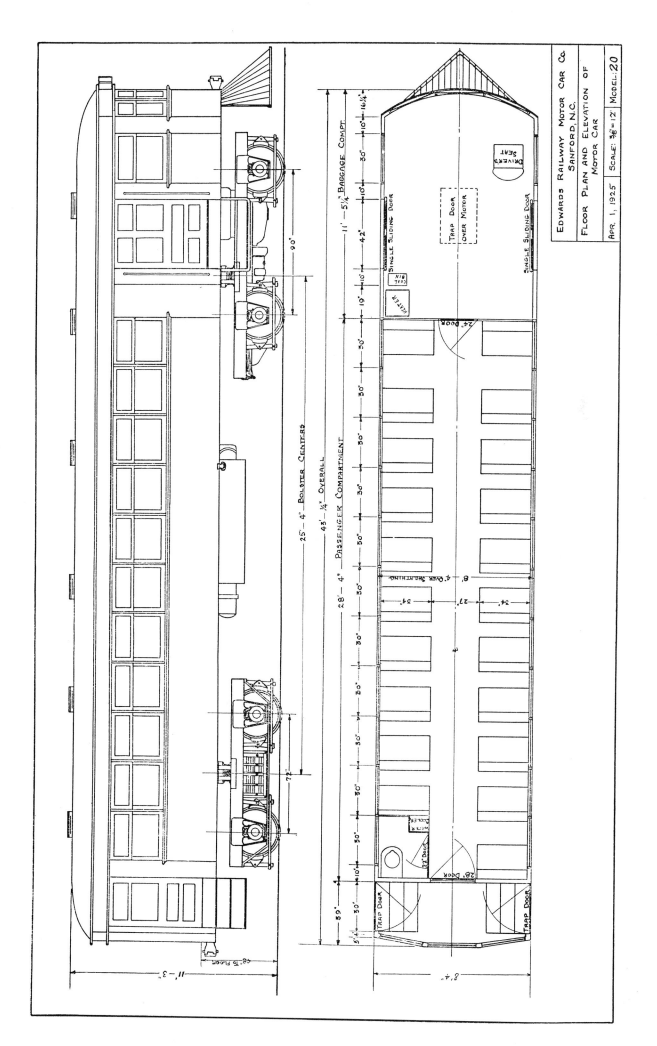

Edwards Railway Motor Car Co.
Sanford, N.C.
Floor Plan and Elevation of Motor Car
Apr. 1, 1925 | Scale: 5/8" = 12" | Model: 20

ED FRIETAS PHOTOGRAPH

Above, Skunk M-200 is pictured as it appeared in the 1960's. Below, the rail bus is shown during its early service on the California Western.

SKUNK M-200

A. E. BARKER COLLECTION

Rail Motor Car M-200 was built by the Skagit Steel and Iron Works of Sedro-Woolley, Washington, in 1927 for the Longview, Portland, and Northern Railway. The rail bus was designated Model 6-46.

The car was powered with a six cylinder Buda 150-horsepower engine carrying the serial number 89144-156636A. It was equipped with Westinghouse air brakes, a two cylinder Westinghouse compressor, and a 12 inch by 46 inch air reservoir.

The vehicle's body was of steel, as was its underframe and rounded roof. Its length including end sills was 44 feet and its width covering side sills was 10 feet. The interior was finished in wood and the car was equipped with a hot water-type heater. One flush toilet was provided. The car was built with seats for 50 passengers. Fully equipped, the rail bus weighed 41,590 pounds.

The car was acquired by the Trona Railway (operating in the Mojave Desert), which sold the vehicle to the California Western Railroad in 1941. The CWR rebuilt the rail car before putting it in operation. The gasoline engine was replaced by a 165 horsepower Cummins diesel plant in 1955 by Watson and Meehan of San Francisco.

Data on the M-200 was provided by S. S. McIntyre, designer of the car; his son, S. S. McIntyre, Jr., president of the Skagit Corporation (successor to the Skagit Steel and Iron works), and in a 1954 report on the vehicle by A. L. Morgan, mechanical superintendent of the Trona Railway, from the collection of A. E. Barker.

Drawings were provided by the Skagit Corporation.

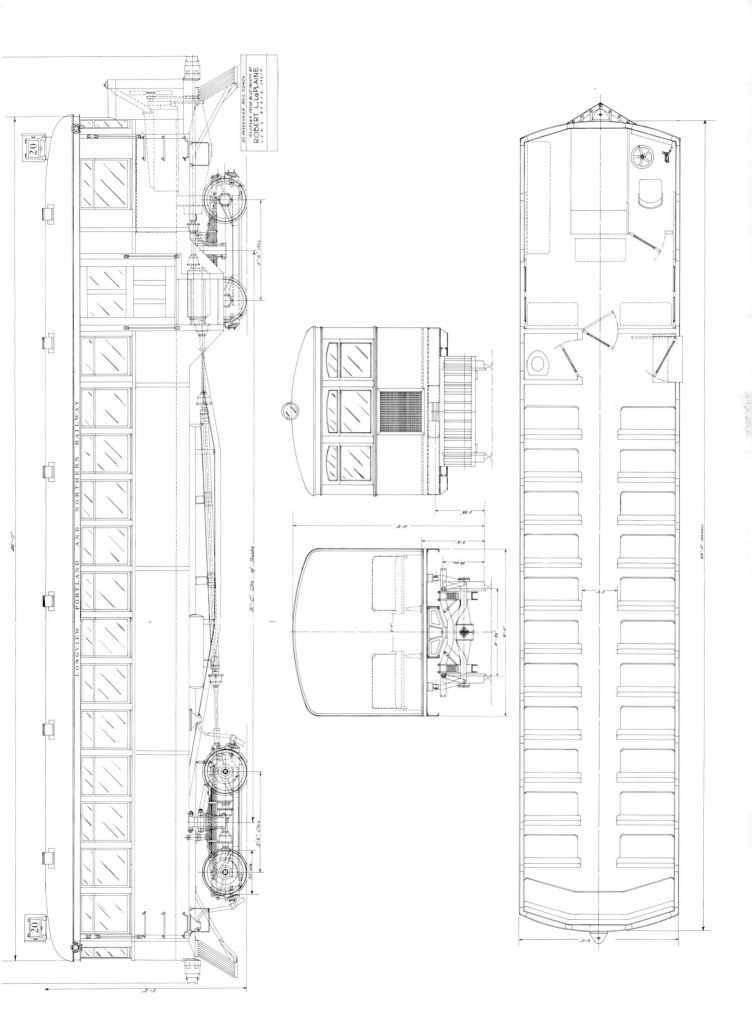

50 PASSENGER RAIL COACH
REDRAWN FROM BLUE PRINTS BY
ROBERT L. LaPLAINE
LONG BEACH, CALIF.

LONGVIEW PORTLAND AND NORTHERN RAILWAY

20

ED FRIETAS PHOTOGRAPH

SKUNK M-300

Rail Motor Car M-300 was built in 1935 by the American Car and Foundry Company of Berwick, Pennsylvania, a producer of railroad passenger coaches and freight cars. The factory equipped the vehicle with a model 180 horizontal Hall-Scott six cylinder engine having a rating of 168 horsepower at 2,200 r.p.m. Its fuel tank had a capacity of 130 gallons of gasoline. The rail bus came with a 12 volt Exide battery.

The vehicle was equipped with 30 inch roller steel wheels and a Westinghouse air brake system. Timken roller journal boxes were provided.

The factory designed the car to seat 57 passengers and equipped it with two toilets, an ACF gas driven air conditioner, and a forced air-water heating system. The baggage compartment was designed to carry 5,000 pounds of cargo. Fully equipped, the rail bus weighed 52,060 pounds.

Serial numbers 2024, 2025 and 2026 were assigned to various cars of this model. The California Western Railroad was unable to determine which number ultimately reached its tracks.

The M-300 saw initial service on the Aberdeen and Rockfish Railroad of North Carolina. It was used later on the Salt Lake, Garfield and Western Saltair route at Salt Lake City. The CWR acquired the vehicle in 1963 and rebuilt it prior to placing it in service. The gasoline engine was replaced by a 220 horsepower Cummins diesel installed by Watson and Meehan of San Francisco.

The historical data and adjoining builder's drawings came from the collection of A. E. Barker.

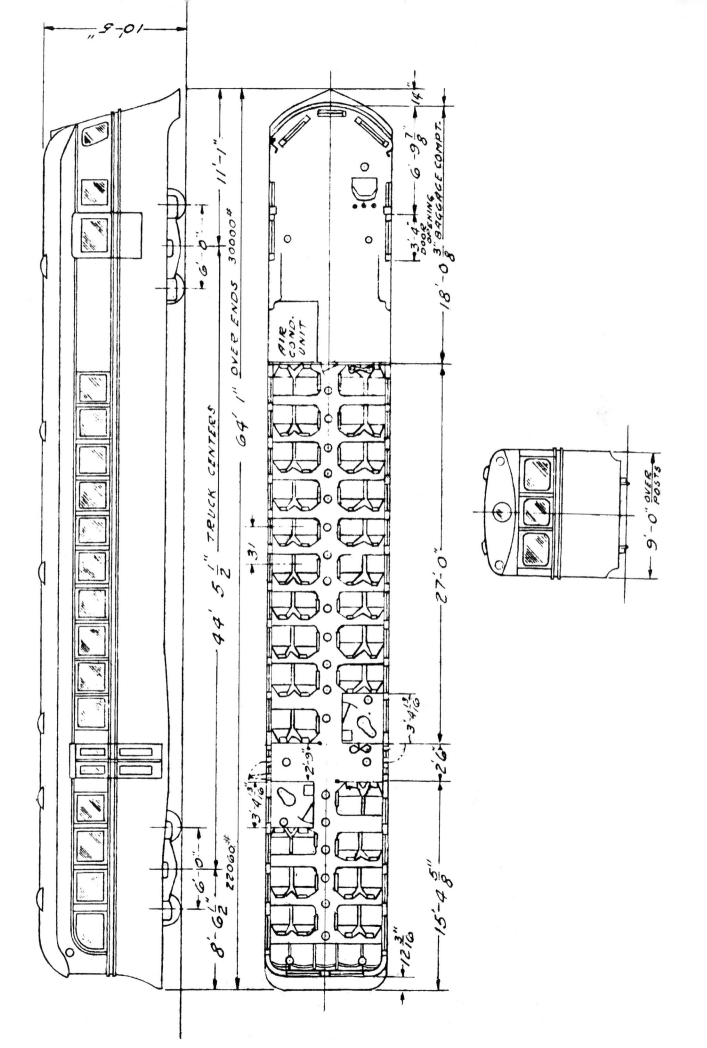

B. Edwards Railway Motor Car Catalog

Following is the reproduction of a 1924 catalog distributed by the Edwards Railway Motor Car Company to railroads as part of a program to attract interest in its rail bus offerings. Motorized rail cars at the time were regarded as an answer to the railroads' problem of declining passenger traffic during the 1920's.

Numerous small companies joined existing manufacturers of rail or bus equipment in offering equipment for the market presumed to be so large. Edwards was one of these firms. It produced the rail car that eventually became California Western Skunk M-100.

The catalog is reproduced through the courtesy of A. E. Barker, of whose collection of railroadiana it is a part.

MONTHLY BULLETIN

EDWARDS RAILWAY MOTOR CAR CO.

SANFORD, NORTH CAROLINA

| VOL. 1 | OCTOBER 1924 | No. 4 |

We wish to here announce to the Railway World that after years of research and experiments, we have now perfected and have ready to put on the market our new model TWIN ENGINE RAILWAY MOTOR CAR, in which we have achieved the IDEAL SELF-PROPELLED RAILWAY CAR, in view of the fact that it has the following outstanding characteristics:

1. This car will maintain a schedule year after year without train failures due to mechanical trouble.

2. This car will never have to be taken into the shop for mechanical repairs.

3. This car will never have to go to he shops for a general over-hauling unless repairs are to be made to the body, such as painting, etc.

4. With the use of this car it will never be necessary to purchase two motor cars or keep a steam train in reserve to protect its schedule runs in event of a mechanical failure.

5. All motor vibration is eliminated from the car body.

6. No universal joints, long drive shafts, angle drives, numerous gears, etc., that predominate in other rail cars are used in the New Edwards Car.

7. No space taken up in the car body for motors.

8. Less moving parts than any other car on the market. Excluding the transmission, only three gears are used in the driving mechanism. We, therefore, have less parts to wear and less parts to repair.

9. Car can be made either single or double end control.

The above results are accomplished in the following manner: In a human being nature provided practically all our vital organs in duplicate and we have followed this plan in our motor car. The car is equipped with two double trucks and we have built one complete power plant into each truck and these power plants will operate independently or together, as desired. If one plant should completely fail, the car will perform with the other power plant. At the option of the purchaser, we furnish with each car, or group of cars operating out of one terminal, an extra power truck and if a mechanical failure occurs, the extra or reserve power truck can be put under the car when it reaches its terminal. This change of trucks can be made in 45 minutes (this was done in an actual test). This extra or reserve power truck can be kept in the shops and maintained in perfect condition at all times ready for any emergency and in this way the motor car can be kept in service continuously, year after year, and it will not be necessary at any time to put it in the shops for any mechanical repairs.

EDWARDS RAILWAY MOTOR CAR CO.
SANFORD, N. C.
U. S. A.

OUR MODEL 25 TWIN ENGINE GASOLINE RAILWAY MOTOR CAR BUILT FOR THE CHICAGO, BURLINGTON AND QUINCY RAILROAD. ONE COMPLETE POWER PLANT IS LOCATED IN EACH TRUCK.

TOTAL WEIGHT OF CAR 39,000 LBS. SEVENTY PER CENT OF THIS WEIGHT IS ON THE DRIVING WHEELS. SEATING CAPACITY 41. BAGGAGE COMPARTMENT 17 FT. LONG. BY 9 FT. 1 IN. WIDE. DETAIL SPECIFICATIONS ON PAGE 12.

TRUCKS

Both front and rear trucks follow closely the conventional four wheel passenger coach type of construction, with such modifications as are necessary to install the power plant. Wheels are 30 inches in diameter rolled steel A. R. A. contour; outside journal boxes are used and are fitted with Hyatt roller bearings; the axles are 4 inches in diameter and made of Chrome nickel steel, heat treated. Coil springs are used over each journal box. One large semi-elliptic spring is located under the bottom bolster.

POWER PLANT

The complete power plant, consisting of radiator, motor, clutch, four speed transmission and reverse mechanism or final drive, are mounted on a sub-frame which is suspended within the regular truck frame by four cantilever springs attached to swing motion hangers. The connection from the final drive to the axle is with two chains running in oil tight housing. This is the Edwards Company patented method of mounting, which permits the frame containing the power plant to move vertically or horizontally and as there is no rigid connection between the driven axle and the power plant frame, all the driving machinery is, therefore, amply protected from all rail shocks and vibration, which is absolutely essential to the life of the machinery in a self propelled car, and especially so when the power plant is put in the trucks. One of these trucks were tested out over an exceptionally rough track at a speed of 35 miles an hour (very high speed for the track used) and no vibration of any consequence could be felt in riding on the sub-frame.

ECONOMY IN FLOOR SPACE AND WEIGHT OF CAR BODY

With the power plant mounted on the truck the motor takes up no space in the car body and some six or nine feet in length of car body saved together with the additional weight that this would add.

ACCESSIBILITY FOR MAKING REPAIRS AND ADJUSTMENTS TO MOTOR, ETC.

Over each motor there is placed a trap door in the floor which permits of easy access to the motor for making all necessary adjustments, removal of cylinder heads, grinding valves, etc. The motors are also easily accessible from the outside of car from each side. Also the truck can be removed from under the car in a very short space of time, and with the truck out the entire power plant is perfectly accessible for all kind of repairs, with the use of any kind of tool, chain hoist, crane, etc.

MOTOR

This truck is so designed that most any motor can be mounted in the same with little difficulty. We are at present prepared to give prompt deliveries on trucks equipped with motors up to 100 horse power.

Cars can be built either with one motor or with two motors as desired by purchaser. On our models 25 and 45 we can use any motor that does not exceed 28 inches high by 52 inches long and on our model 35 we can use considerably larger motors. The size of motor to be used should be determined by the service the car is to perform.

FLEXIBILITY

In this new Edwards Car you have a very flexible type of construction, in the fact that its power can be readily increased or decreased as desired. For instance, cars can be furnished with power plant in only one truck and should the car be put in heavier service, later on an additional power

INTERIOR VIEW OF CAR MODEL 25

ELECTRICAL EQUIPMENT

A Kohler automatic light and power plant is installed in the driver's cab. This plant furnishes 110 volts D. C. current for operating the lights of the car, driving the air compressor and operating the motors of the heating system. The Kohler plant has 2500 watt capacity and is driven by a small three horse power four cylinder motor. This plant is very compact and occupies a floor space of only 15 in. x 33 in. These plants are used for farm lighting and on boats. Repair parts or duplicate plants can be obtained in any large city. We, therefore, take no power at all from the motor driving the car for operating the air compressor, lights or other electrical appliances used.

In addition to the above electric plant, the driving motors are equipped with a generator, self starter and a storage battery. This system will also supply current to several auxiliary lamps located in the car for emergency use. The car is equipped with a powerful 240 watt headlight.

BRAKES

A complete set of Standard Westinghouse Air Brakes are installed on the car, which brake system is the straight air with emergency feature. The air compressor is of the regular standard street car type operated by the electric power plant described in the above paragraph. The automatic air brake equipment can be installed if desired.

In addition to this air brake system, there is an efficient hand brake system operated by a ratchet located convenient to the driver.

SYNCHRONIZING MOTORS

In view of the fact that the motors drive to separate axles and are in no way connected except through the rails, it is not necessary that the motors be perfectly synchronized. Through our control system the motors are synchronized near enough for all practical purposes. In the operation of this car no loss of power can be detected due to any failure of perfect motor synchronization. It is possible to cut either motor in or out while the car is in motion without he slightest difficulty.

SPEED

When 75 horse motors are used, a maximum speed of 45 miles per hour can be obtained on level track and with 100 horse power motors 55 to 60 miles per hour. The car will operate at the same speed in both forward or backward directions and has 4 speed changes or gear reductions in both directions.

OTHER EQUIPMENT

The equipment used in our power plants are all of standard design made by reputable manufacturers, such as Stromberg carburetor, Eisemann magnetor, Cotta transmission, Buda, Waukesha and Continental motors, Westinghouse electric equipment and the like. Therefore, service can be readily obtained on any of these vital parts throughout the country. Bolts and nuts used are U. S. Standard..

EDWARDS RAILWAY MOTOR CAR CO.
SANFORD. N. C.
U. S. A.

Patents Applied For

REAR AND SIDE VIEW OF POWER TRUCK

THE CAR BODY

Our car body, as illustrated in this pamphlet, is constructed of steel with wood inside finish. The center sills are eight inch 20.5 pound I Beams. The side sills are 3/8 x 3 1/2 x 6" steel angles, cross members press steel shapes. The side posts are steel tees 1/4 x 1 3/4 x 1 3/4". These tees also form the car lines and are in one continuous piece, running from side sill to side sill. The corner posts are formed from 12 gauge steel and run from side sill to letter panel. The side sheeting and letter panel is 16 gauge patent leveled copper bearing steel. The letter panel extends about 6 in. back on top of the roof and is flanged down to form a stiffner for the roof.

The roof is of the turtle back type, extending full length of car. Roof boards are 3/8 x 2 1/2 tongue and groved poplar dressed to a smooth surface painted and covered with 8 lb. canvas bedded in white lead.

The floor is laid with yellow pine of double thickness with a deadening felt in between the layers.

The inside finish, consisting of doors, sash, partitions and panels below rail is birch stained natural mahogany.

OTHER EQUIPMENT

The car is equipped with one toilet with dry hopper and Dayton sanitary water cooler. Parcel racks are provided in the passenger compartment and run the full length on both sides over the seats.

The seats are of the non-reversible type with pressed steel pedestals, wall and aisle plates, upholstered in leather. The seats on one side of the aisle are 52 in. wide for three passengers and 34 in. wide on the other side for two passengers. This leaves a 23 in. aisle way through the car.

Attractive electric light fixtures are provided throughout the car. A curtain is provided at each window. All windows and doors are fitted with the best quality of coach hardware. Other equipment consists of signal bell, air sanders, alarm bell operated by air, electric classification lamps, fire extinguishers and Peter Smith hot air heating system.

DIMENSIONS OF CAR BODY

The car here illustrated is 43 ft. long, 9 1/2 ft. wide and 8 ft. high from floor to ceiling. The height from top of rail to floor level is 51 in., made so to fit up with standard equipment. We are prepared to build these cars in the following lengths: 43 feet, 50 feet and 55 feet, all 9 ft. 6 in. wide, and in view of the fact that no space is taken up in the body of the car for motors our cars give more revenue space than other cars of same lengths.

COUPLERS, ETC.

Special light weight standard M. C. B. couplers are provided at both ends of the car, fixed at standard draw bar heights. Also necessary grab handles, steps, etc. to comply with I. C. C. requirements.

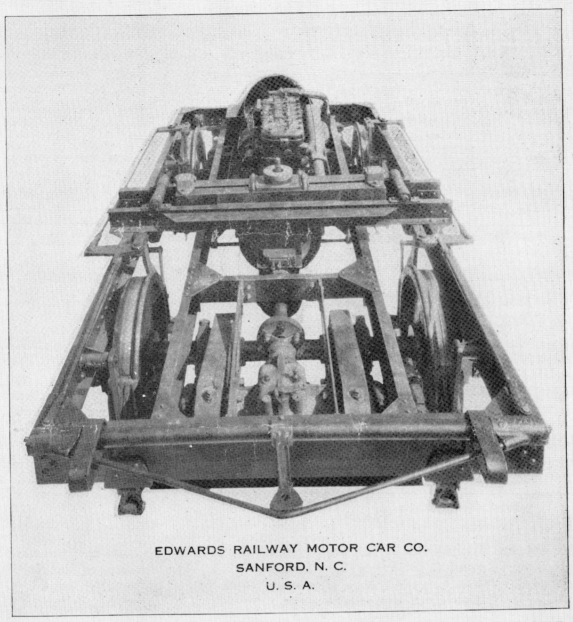

EDWARDS RAILWAY MOTOR CAR CO.
SANFORD, N. C.
U. S. A.

Patents Applied For

Top view of power truck. Note the absence of long drive shafts,
universal joints, angle drives, numerous gears, etc., that predominate in
other rail cars. Our power from the motor is delivered to the driving
wheels with the lowest possible loss of efficiency.

EDWARDS RAILWAY MOTOR CAR CO.
SANFORD, N. C.
U. S. A.

View of side, roof and underframe construction of our car bodies. Note the substantial nature of this construction, detail description of same on page 9.

CONDENSED SPECIFICATIONS OF C. B. & Q. CAR No. 502.

POWER PLANT

MOTOR: Two Buda four cylinder 5 in. bore, 6½ in. stroke, 60 horse power each at 1200 R. P. M.

CARBURETOR: Stromberg.

MAGNETO: Eisemann.

CLUTCH: Detlaff multiple disc, especially designed for heavy duty work.

TRANSMISSION: Cotta four speed constant mesh type, for heavy duty work. Same number of speed changes both forward or backward directions.

FINAL DRIVE: Edwards special final drive and reverse mechanism.

RADIATORS: Edwards special design; constructed of copper sheets and tubes, arranged for cooling motor in both forward or backward directions.

TRUCKS

GAUGE: Standard 4 ft. 8½".

WHEEL BASE: Seven and one-half feet.

WHEELS: Roller steel 30 inch diameter A. R. A. contour. wheels are pressed on axles.

AXLES: Heat treated Chrome nickel steel 4 inch diameter journals 3¼" x 5½"

JOURNAL BOXES: Semi-steel, located outside of wheels for convenient access for oiling or renewal of bearings.

JOURNAL BEARINGS: Hyatt roller bearings, standard railroad type.

SPRINGS: Four coil springs over journal boxes, one large semi-elliptic spring in bottom bolster, four cantileter springs supporting power plant (Edwards patented mounting).

FRAME: Truck and power plant frame is made of 8 in. steel channels, gusset plates, steel shapes, etc., all hot rivited together.

PEDESTALS: Cast steel, machined to receive journal box.

BODY

DIMENSIONS: Length over body 42 ft. 11¼ in.   Height rail to top of car 12 ft. 4 in.
Width over sheathing 9 ft. 6 in.   Height rail to floor 4 ft. 3 in.
Height floor to ceiling 8 ft. 0 in.   Bolster centers 25 ft. 6 in.

CONSTRUCTION: Substantial steel construction throughout with wood interior finish.

BAGGAGE COMPARTMENT: 17 ft. long 9 ft. 1 in. wide. Inside ceiled with Birch finished natural mahogany. Two 44 in. doors, one on each side of car.

PASSENGER COMPARTMENT: 22 ft. 7 in. long by 9 ft. 1 in. wide. Inside finished in Birch stained natural mahogany. Birch panels below belt rails, ceiling car line finish painted Ivory enamel. Seats provided for 41 passengers. Seats are 52 in. wide on one side of aisle and 34 in. wide on other, each seating three and two passengers, respectively. Upholstering leather.

TOILET: One located in passenger compartment, equipped with dry hopper and Dayton sanitary water cooler.

REAR PLATFORM: Enclosed vestibule, pullman type, trap doors over steps.

COUPLERS: Standard light weight M. C. B. couplers on each end of car.

HEATING: Peter Smith hot air heater located in baggage compartment and heat distributed throughout the car with hot air ducts.

GASOLINE TANK: One 65 gallon gasoline tank is located under the car body arranged for convenient filling from the outside. This tank supplies fuel to both motors.

OTHER EQUIPMENT: Air whistle, air operated alarm bell, air sanders, electric lights, 240 watt locomotive headlight, steel pilot.

EDWARDS RAILWAY MOTOR CAR CO.

625 Canadian Pacific Bldg.
NEW YORK CITY

637 Mission Street, Rialto Bldg.
SAN FRANCISCO, CAL.

Offices at
Fisher Building
CHICAGO, ILL.
GENERAL OFFICE:
SANFORD, NORTH CAROLINA

Barth Building
DENVER, COL.

630 Louisiana Avenue,
WASHINGTON, D. C.

BILL PENNINGTON COLLECTION

Adjoining is a table listing information pertinent to the financial operations of the California Western Railroad. The data is based on reports filed with the California Public Utilities Commission (previously the California Railroad Commission).

The entries regarding passengers cover all passengers carried, including loggers. Items under the "expenses" category include wages, maintenance operations, and related expenditures.

The entry of an asterisk (*) indicates that the information was not available.

JAMES GAYNER COLLECTION

Year	Number of Passengers Carried	Passenger Revenue	Total Revenue	Expenses	Net or (Loss)
1909	*	*	$113,691	$ 90,490	$ 23,200
1910	*	*	155,573	125,741	29,832
1911	*	$30,942	152,155	99,093	54,062
1912	*	37,422	208,372	102,512	105,512
1913	*	60,126	299,653	241,004	58,649
1914	*	64,578	265,376	166,656	80,931
1915	28,585	52,426	233,818	206,747	27,071
1916	31,615	58,654	258,411	184,445	73,966
1917	*	63,765	261,365	214,796	46,569
1918	19,079	59,641	281,272	215,490	65,782
1919	32,465	67,787	287,170	242,830	44,340
1920	34,585	81,942	279,296	245,475	33,821
1921	33,832	86,248	336,331	285,279	51,052
1922	36,240	79,035	300,984	253,143	47,841
1923	38,822	75,276	306,156	258,193	47,963
1924	32,299	63,705	260,691	235,853	24,838
1925	29,761	54,450	274,680	217,217	57,463
1926	28,112	51,932	253,559	221,570	31,989
1927	23,025	47,616	245,653	228,836	16,817
1928	20,097	34,767	209,962	198,399	11,563
1929	16,824	26,516	212,477	193,867	18,610
1930	13,056	16,823	173,057	156,064	16,993
1931	8,720	10,533	145,266	120,638	24,628
1932	8,772	8,149	120,165	108,697	11,468
1933	18,464	9,078	136,734	116,806	19,928
1934	25,626	14,451	164,137	159,991	4,146
1935	32,566	15,984	209,962	206,195	3,767
1936	23,254	12,656	221,631	209,340	12,291
1937	10,507	10,538	223,586	219,943	3,643
1938	12,094	10,834	199,102	219,568	(20,466)
1939	13,602	9,148	245,566	244,787	779
1940	12,556	8,825	287,618	262,350	25,268
1941	15,076	9,320	310,043	258,043	52,000
1942	14,560	8,325	379,523	324,391	55,132
1943	7,844	5,940	398,718	335,382	63,336
1944	9,018	4,579	367,530	353,283	14,247
1945	13,717	6,616	337,672	363,146	(25,474)
1946	16,607	9,740	171,472	206,633	(35,161)
1947	17,246	11,348	368,605	340,086	28,519
1948	17,246	11,515	540,702	491,252	49,450
1949	18,080	12,947	400,155	398,428	1,727
1950	17,187	13,221	516,438	465,826	50,612
1951	19,700	12,992	553,168	533,246	19,922
1952	14,427	10,723	550,445	507,410	43,035
1953	13,440	11,354	565,182	533,169	32,013
1954	16,308	14,433	554,506	610,262	(55,756)
1955	22,097	21,947	601,004	609,546	(8,542)
1956	14,923	17,752	624,934	603,598	21,336
1957	16,223	21,829	571,103	582,157	(11,054)
1958	22,598	32,334	579,353	572,776	6,577
1959	37,624	57,860	675,301	652,858	22,443
1960	39,414	60,977	608,011	614,631	(6,620)
1961	44,359	69,349	694,335	667,823	26,512
1962	43,419	68,419	726,923	693,425	33,498

D. Fort Bragg Railroad Articles of Incorporation

Following are the articles of incorporation for the Fort Bragg Railroad Company, filed April 30, 1885, with the California Secretary of State. The railroad was the immediate predecessor of the California-Western Railroad and Navigation Company. Its officers also served as directors of the Fort Bragg Lumber Company, predecessor of the Union Lumber Company.

The properties of the Fort Bragg Railroad were absorbed by the California-Western on its formation in 1905.

ARTICLES OF INCORPORATION OF THE FORT BRAGG RAILROAD COMPANY

KNOW ALL MEN BY THESE PRESENTS, that we, the undersigned, have this day voluntarily associated ourselves together for the purpose of forming a corporation, under the laws of the State of California, and we hereby certify:

FIRST: That the name of said corporation is Fort Bragg Railroad Company.

SECOND: That the purposes for which it is formed are constructing, conducting, maintaining, and operating a railroad with cars to be propelled by steam with all the side tracks, switches, and appurtenances, necessary, and convenient therefore.

THIRD: That the place where its principal business is to be transacted shall be the City and County of San Francisco, State of California.

FOURTH: That the term for which it is to exist is fifty years from and after the date of its incorporation.

FIFTH: That the number of its directors shall be six and that the names and residences of those who are appointed for the first year are:

SIXTH: That the amount of the capital stock of this corporation shall be two hundred thousand dollars divided into two thousand shares of the par value of one hundred dollars each.

SEVENTH: That the amount of said capital stock which has been actually subscribed is thirty thousand dollars.

EIGHTH: That the kind of road intended to be constructed is standard or narrow gauge steam railroad.

NINTH: That said railroad is intended to be run from the tide water of Fort Bragg Harbor in Mendocino County, State of California, in an easterly direction to the head waters of the Noyo River in said county, an estimated distance of twenty miles, with a branch connecting with said road at a point about four miles from the terminus at Fort Bragg Harbor and running in a north easterly direction to a point on Ten Mile River and the estimated length of said branch road is ten miles.

TENTH: That the following are the names of the persons by whom the capital stock has been subscribed, to wit:

Name	No. Shares	Amount
Otis R. Johnson	200	$20,000
John C. Huggins	20	2,000
Charles R. Johnson	20	2,000
Calvin Stewart	20	2,000
Charles E. Wilson	20	2,000
James Hunter	20	2,000

ELEVENTH: That ten per cent of the capital stock subscribed has been paid into Charles R. Johnson, who has been elected treasurer of said intended corporation by the subscribers.

IN WITNESS WHEREOF, we have hereunto set our hands and seals this thirteenth day of April, 1885.

Otis R. Johnson
John C. Huggins
Charles E. Wilson
Calvin Stewart
Charles R. Johnson
James Hunter

Names	Residences
Otis R. Johnson	Racine, Wisconsin
John C. Huggins	San Francisco, California
Charles E. Wilson	San Francisco, California
Calvin Stewart	Kibesillah, California
Charles R. Johnson	Kibesillah, California
James Hunter	Vallejo, California

Below are the articles of incorporation for the California-Western Railroad and Navigation Company as filed June 30, 1905, with the California Secretary of State. The firm succeeded the Fort Bragg Railroad Company, which started operations in 1885.

Effective January 1, 1948, the corporate name was shortened to California Western Railroad. The hyphen had been removed unofficially in popular usage for many years. This firm itself never operated ships, but based its title of "navigation" on control of wharf rights at Fort Bragg.

ARTICLES OF INCORPORATION OF THE CALIFORNIA-WESTERN RAILROAD & NAVIGATION COMPANY

KNOW ALL MEN BY THESE PRESENTS: That we, the undersigned, a majority of whom are citizens and residents of the State of California, have this day voluntarily associated ourselves together for the purpose of forming a railroad corporation under the laws of the State of California.

AND WE HEREBY CERTIFY AS FOLLOWS, TO-WIT:

FIRST: That the name of said corporation shall be "CALIFORNIA-WESTERN RAILROAD & NAVIGATION COMPANY."

SECOND: That the purpose for which said corporation is formed are as follows, namely:

To acquire, purchase, construct, own, control, conduct, maintain and operate a steam railroad in the County of Mendocino, State of California, for the transportation of freight and passengers for hire; together with such side tracks, spurs, switch-tracks and switches as may be necessary or convenient to enable said corporation to conduct and carry on its business, and to reach mills and towns along or near its main line or branches; and as incidental thereto acquire by condemnation proceedings, purchase or otherwise such property real or personal as may be necessary for the purpose of such railroad, and exercise the right of eminent domain; To acquire, purchase, conduct, hold, own, use, lease, hire, improve, exchange, deal and trade in real estate, coal, stone and other minerals, franchises, licenses, easements, rights of way, bonds and securities of either private, public or quasi-public corporations, patent rights, inventions, and personal property of all kinds, natures and descriptions; To borrow money, issue bonds, promissory notes and other evidences of indebtedness; bargain, sell, exchange, transfer, convey, mortgage, hypothecate, pledge or otherwise purpose of such railroad, and exercise the right of eminent which said corporation may acquire or own; To subscribe for, purchase, acquire, receive in exchange for its own stock or other property, hold, own, pledge, sell, exchange and dispose of capital stock or shares of capital stock in other corporations of all kinds, and to have and exercise all of the rights and privileges of a stockholder in such corporation or corporations; To guarantee bonds of other corporations whose stock or property, or any part thereof, may become the property of this corporation; to manage and conduct pleasure resorts or grounds in connection with the business of said railroad, and to operate, manage, conduct or carry on any and all kinds of other business in which it may be deemed profitable to engage in connection with or incidental to the purposes hereinbefore expressed; and to enter into all lawful contractual relations with other persons, firms, associations or corporations for any and all purposes.

To acquire, hold, own, buy, sell, manage, control, improve and operate wharves, booms, piers, and chutes; and wharf, boom, pier and chute franchises and privileges; to acquire, buy, sell, hold, own, charter, manage, control and operate steam boats, ships and vessels, and other craft propelled by steam or otherwise; and navigate the waters of the rivers, streams, bays and oceans with said vessels, and carry on the business of a common carrier.

To do and perform any and all acts which may be either necessary, proper or convenient in or incidental to carrying out any and all of the purposes for which this corporation is formed as aforesaid.

THIRD: That the places from which and to which said railroad is intended to be run, and all its intermediate branches, are as follows, to-wit: Commencing at tide water on the shore of the Pacific Ocean at the City of Fort Bragg in Mendocino County, State of California, and running thence in an Easterly direction over and along the present route of the railroad now operated by Union Lumber Company to the Noyo River; thence up and along said River over and upon the route of said Union Lumber Company's said railroad, as now constructed and operated, to the present Easterly terminus thereof at Alpine; thence up and along said Noyo River over the most practicable route to the divide between the water shed of the Noyo River and Little Lake Valley; thence leaving said Noyo River and running in an Easterly direction along the most practicable route to a point in or near the City of Willits in Townships Eighteen (18) North; Ranges Thirteen (13) and Fourteen (14) West, Mount Diablo Base and Meridian, the estimated length of which is forty-one (41) miles; with intermediate branches from said main line as above described as follows, to-wit:

(a) Commencing at the junction of what is known as Pudding Creek Branch of said Union Lumber Company's railroad with said Main line in Section Four (4), Township Eighteen (18) North, Range Seventeen (17) West, Mount Diablo Base and Meridian, and running thence over and upon the route of said Union Lumber Company's railroad as now constructed up and along said Pudding Creek to the

Northerly terminus of said Union Lumber Company's railroad at the Town of Glen Blair in Section Thirty-five (35), Township Nineteen (19) North, Range Seventeen (17) West, Mount Diablo Base and Meridian, the estimated length of which is three (3) miles.

(b) Commencing at a point on the main line of said railroad first above described at or near the junction of the North Fork of the Noyo River with the main Noyo River in Section Seventeen (17), Township Eighteen (18) North, Range Fifteen (15) West, Mount Diablo Base and Meridian, then running up and along said North Fork in a Northerly direction over and upon the most practicable route to the divide between the water shed of the Noyo River and Sherwood Valley; thence leaving said North Fork and running in a Northerly direction over and along the most practicable route to a point in or near the Town of Sherwood situated in Township Nineteen (19) North, Range Fourteen (14) West, Mount Diablo Base and Meridian, the estimated length of which is twenty (20) miles.

(c) Commencing at a point on the main line of said railroad first above described in said City of Fort Bragg, which point is the present junction of what is known as the Noyo Branch of the Union Lumber Company's railroad with said main line, and running thence Southerly over and along the route of said branch road as now used and operated by said Union Lumber Company to the terminus of said branch road at the shore of the Pacific Ocean, the estimated length of which is one (1) mile.

That the estimated length of said railroad, with its intermediate branches, is sixty-five (65) miles.

FOURTH: That the place where the principal business of said corporation is to be transacted is the City and County of San Francisco, State of California.

FIFTH: That the term for which said corporation is to exist is fifty (50) years from and after the date of its incorporation.

SIXTH: That the amount of the capital stock of the corporation shall be One Million (1,000,000) Dollars, and the number of shares into which it is divided is Ten Thousand (10,000) of the par value of One Hundred (100) Dollars each.

SEVENTH: That the number of directors of said corporation shall be five (5). That the names and residences of the directors who are appointed for the first year, and to serve until their successors have been elected and qualified, are as follows, to-wit:

Names	Residences
Duncan McNee	San Francisco, California.
Miles W. McIntosh	San Francisco, California.
Chas. H. Weller	San Francisco, California.
H. M. Cochran	San Francisco, California.
Max Goldberg	San Francisco, California.

EIGHTH: That the amount of capital stock which has actually been subscribed is Sixty-five Thousand (65,000) Dollars, and the following are the names of the persons by whom the same has been subscribed, to-wit:

Names	No. shares	Amount
W. P. Plummer	625	$62,500.00
Duncan McNee	5	500.00
Miles W. McIntosh	5	500.00
Chas. H. Weller	5	500.00
H. M. Cochran	5	500.00
Max Goldberg	5	500.00

That at least ten (10) per cent thereof has been paid to the Treasurer of the corporation, who was duly elected by the subscribers; and that Chas. H. Weller has been elected Treasurer of said intended corporation until the Board of Directors order otherwise.

IN WITNESS WHEREOF, we have hereunto set our hands and seals this 29th day of June, 1905.

W. P. PLUMMER
DUNCAN McNEE
MILES W. McINTOSH
CHAS. H. WELLER
MAX GOLDBERG
H. M. COCHRAN

ED FRIETAS PHOTOGRAPHS

Passengers gather to look at the "Super Skunk," which brought the return of steam service to the Redwood Route. Popularity of the line increases annually.

The Appendix:
STEAM ROLLS AGAIN!

While many American railroads were reducing service, the California Western marked the 1970's as a time to increase its scope of operations.

The happy days of steam passenger service returned to the CWR in the summer of 1965. Resumption of this conventional rail operation not only provided a thrill to those riding on the spectacular Redwood Route. It also meant that many people previously unable to take the trip because of the crowded Skunk rail buses would have better chances to ride.

Steam passenger service seemed like something relegated to history following the retirement of the California Western's passenger coaches "42" and "43" in 1949 and the 1956 sales of its last locomotive, No. 14. With steam locomotives gone, diesel engines took over the duties of hauling freight. The Skunk rail cars carried all passengers, and in doing so gained an increasing amount of international fame.

The beautiful Redwood Route gained in fame, too, and more and more people came to ride over it.

The four Skunks, with seating capacities totalling approximately 200 passengers, could hardly carry all of the people who came to enjoy the route. Even though the faithful rail buses made additional trips on busy days during the peak of the summer seasons, the increasing popularity of the line brought so many visitors that some prospective passengers had to wait another day to make the trip because of limited seating capacities.

The virtual destruction of Skunk M-80 in the 1964 accident (see pages 104 and 105) caused it to be placed out of service indefinitely, making the other rail buses even busier.

When all four rail buses were operating in 1964, they carried 69,045 passengers — double the number of just five years before. A year later, with the M-80 out of service, passenger volume soared to 77,856 — an all-time high.

The help from steam power that arrived in 1965 was most welcome.

The steam locomotive which went into service on July 1, 1965, was a Baldwin Mikado. Similar to the California Western's Engine No. 44, it was built in 1924 for the Brownlee-Olds Lumber Company of Medford, Oregon. The CWR purchased the locomotive from the firm's successor, The Medford Corporation, which had used the engine as late as 1959.

The decision to resume steam locomotive service was not based entirely on the line's increasing passenger volume. CWR officials said that the return of the Iron Horse to the Redwood Route also came so that the public could enjoy a nostalgic taste of the glory days of railroading.

"We felt that the steam locomotive was part of our heritage," explained R. A. Regalia, the CWR's assistant general manager and auditor, who — with Clair W. MacLeod and F. H. Sturges, president and vice

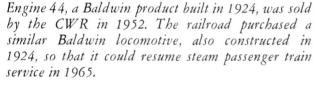

Engine 44, a Baldwin product built in 1924, was sold by the CWR in 1952. The railroad purchased a similar Baldwin locomotive, also constructed in 1924, so that it could resume steam passenger train service in 1965.

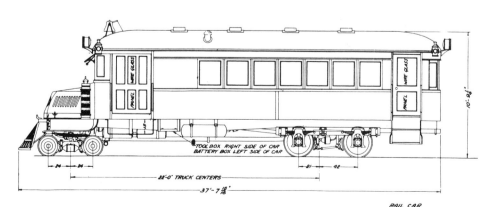

TOOL BOX RIGHT SIDE OF CAR
BATTERY BOX LEFT SIDE OF CAR

22'-0" TRUCK CENTERS

37'-7 13/16"

10'-9 1/2"

RAIL CAR

163

ED FRIETAS PHOTOGRAPHS

The "Super Skunk" prepares to leave the station at Fort Bragg after loading its capacity of passengers.

THE IRON HORSE
RETURNS TO THI

A candy butcher provides refreshments on a coach pulled by a steam locomotive over the CWR's Redwood Route.

CALIFORNIA WESTERN

RAILROAD

STEAM TRAIN will not stop at intermediate stations for the purpose of receiving or letting off passengers.

SKUNKS (Rail Cars) will stop at intermediate stations for the purpose of receiving or letting off passengers, upon being flagged.

RESERVATIONS: Requests for reservations will be accepted only by mail addressed to "Reservation Desk", California Western Railroad, Fort Bragg, California, Zip Code 95437, or in person at the Station of departure. No telephone reservations will be accepted. Total fare must accompany request for reservations. Requests for reservations must be in the hands of the California Western Railroad not earlier than 90 days prior to departure date and not later than 8 AM the day before departure.

SCHEDULES AND EQUIPMENT: Management reserves the right to change schedules and substitute equipment without notice.

CAMP SUPPLIES AND PARCELS will be handled in Skunks (Rail Cars) only. Tariff Rates will apply.

SERVICE CHARGE of 25¢ will be made on redemption of each unused ticket, or change of reservation made within 72 hours of original reservation date.

FARES: Fort Bragg-Willits - 90 Day Roundtrip $4.50; One Way $3.00. Children 5 thru 11 incl., One-half fare; under 5-yrs. free, except when occupying a seat.

CALIFORNIA WESTERN RAILROAD

RESERVATION REQUEST

Send reserved tickets for _____ adults
and _____ children.

Date: 1st _____   2nd _____
(Give 2 choices)

☐ ROUNDTRIP

☐ ONE WAY

Leave from Fort Bragg (Time) _____

Return to Fort Bragg (Time) _____

****

Leave from Willits (Time) _____

Return to Willits (Time) _____

$_____ enclosed. (See time table for fares)

PLEASE PRINT CLEARLY

Name _____

Address_____

City _____ Zip _____

State _____

IMPORTANT: MAIL REQUEST EARLY OR SPACE MAY NOT BE AVAILABLE.

When passenger traffic increased, the California Western produced forms such as this so that travelers could make advance reservations to assure seats.

166

The summer season brings capacity crowds to the California Western. These railroad employees are processing reservations made by prospective passengers who wished to be assured of seats.

president respectively — helped select the equipment. Obtaining a serviceable steam locomotive at a time when most such engines had been scrapped proved a problem. The CWR officials received assistance from several rail fans during the search.

The California Western rebuilt the locomotive in its Fort Bragg yards.

The need for passenger coaches was solved with the purchase of four commuter cars built in 1926 by the Standard Steel Car Company for the Erie Railroad. The CWR acquired the coaches from the Erie's

successor, the Erie-Lackawanna, which operated them as numbers 2300, 2332, 2343, and 2344. The coaches, 72'7½" long, each provided 84 seats. This gave the train a capacity of 326 passengers.

PICTURE FOLLOWING:
Locomotive 45, providing "Super Skunk" steam service, and Skunk M-300 pose while carrying passengers over the scenic route between Fort Bragg and Willits.

ED FRIETAS PHOTOGRAPHS

ABOVE: Engine 46 is pictured as it went into "Super Skunk" service in 1970 after being overhauled by the California Western. The engine was acquired to help haul more passengers.

This is Rayonier Locomotive III, pictured soon after its arrival in Fort Bragg. The engine, after being overhauled, went into California Western service in 1970 as Locomotive 46. It was acquired because of the increasing popularity of "Super Skunk" passenger service.

sengers took the steam train. The Skunk railroad's fame spread even more, and by 1968 the steam train carried 72,614 passengers while the rail buses took 52,499 riders. The total of 125,113 passengers that rode the Redwood Route that year would have been unbelievable a decade before, when less than 25,000 people rode on the line annually.

The CWR's revived steam passenger train obvi-

ously was something super, and it deserved a name to set it aside from ordinary rail service.

Appropriately, CWR officials named the new steam train "Super Skunk."

The Super Skunk was something to bring pleased smiles from young and old.

Forsaking conventional all-black motive equipment and drab olive coaches, the Super Skunk sparkled with color, as did the famous trains of a century ago. Red, with yellow trimming, adorned the sides of the locomotive cab and the passenger coaches.

Puffing and chugging over the Redwood Route, the colorful train looked like something lifted from the nineteenth century — or a movie spectacle depicting that nostalgic era.

More and more people came to ride, and even the Super Skunk needed help!

CWR executives began to search for another steam locomotive, and in 1968 located one at the Rayonier timber operations near Hoquiam, Washington. The Baldwin-built Mallet was constructed in 1937 for the Weyerhaeuser Lumber Company, which sold it to Rayonier.

The 62-foot locomotive was overhauled in the CWR's Fort Bragg shops, designated "No. 46," and placed into Redwood Route service in the summer of 1970.

Meanwhile, the CWR's parent firm, the Union

The fate of Skunk M-80, pictured beginning a down-grade on the CWR route, was in question following a 1964 accident that virtually destroyed the pictur-esque rail bus.

DONALD DUKE

The Wabash diesel No. 307 went into operation in 1968 as California Western Locomotive 54. A working railroad, the California Western carries freight as well as passengers.

Lumber Company, was acquired in 1969 by a growing corporate conglomerate, the Boise-Cascade Corporation.

There was every reason to believe that the California Western would continue to operate, serving as an effective public relations tool as well as an important source of income to the Fort Bragg economy through the vast numbers of visitors attracted.

The California Western's owners have believed, fortunately, in preserving the rail heritage despite economic pinches. The line, price-marked at approximately $2 million in 1912, would cost many times

ALL ABOARD FOR THE

Even though steam trains went into operation, the faithful Skunk rail cars continued to operate. M-300 goes over a redwood-shaded bridge.

REDWOOD ROUTE!

ED FRIETAS PHOTOGRAPHS

"Super Skunk" steam service, launched in 1965, resembles the service provided during the CWR era of the 1900's, although the train is painted red.

that amount to duplicate today. It never was a bonanza to its owners (see pages 156 and 157). Even with more passengers, profits have not climbed sharply. The CWR's gross in 1963 was $800,000 (including $69,045 from Skunk fares), but profits came to only $45,692. The 1969 gross of approximately $990,000 included passenger fares reaching a whopping $240,000, but the profit hit only $55,000.

The views along the California Western's Redwood Route, of course, will remain priceless through the ages.

John Pimentel — the man from the Azores who arrived at Fort Bragg when the twentieth century was young, became a crew member on the first passenger train from Fort Bragg to Willits, and remained to make his home near the redwoods he loved — stated it most correctly.

"The grandeur of the redwoods will unfold," he said, "in majesty unduplicated in pictures as the people ride our railroad through the Big Trees."

More and more people will see the greatness of the redwoods as steam trains and rail buses roll through the forest where the silence is broken only by a whistle.